# Rumi's Tales
## from the Silk Road

# Rumi's Tales
## from the Silk Road

## A Pilgrimage to Paradise

Kamla K. Kapur

MANDALA
PUBLISHING

*San Rafael, California*

**MANDALA**
PUBLISHING

Mandala Publishing
3160 Kerner Blvd., Unit 108
San Rafael, CA 94901
www.mandalapublishing.com
800.688.2218

www.kamlakkapur.com

Library of Congress Cataloging-in-Publication Data available.

ISBN: 978-1-60109-049-2

ROOTS of PEACE    ⊕ REPLANTED PAPER

Roots of Peace is an internationally renowned humanitarian organization dedicated to
eradicating landmines worldwide and converting war-torn lands into productive farms and
wildlife habitats. Together, we will plant two million fruit and nut trees in Afghanistan and
provide farmers there with the skills and support necessary for sustainable land use.

Printed in China by
Palace Press International.
www.palacepress.com

10 9 8 7 6 5 4 3 2 1

*To the Pirs of Islam*
*Who knew how to walk*
*the Way*

# Table of Contents

# Author's Preface

AM A LOVER OF RUMI, rather than a scholar of his work. These stories are a labor of love. And indeed, the labor has been considerable, joyous, and immensely rewarding. The source of these stories, Rumi's six-volume *Mathnawi*, written in Persian and rendered into English by Reynold A. Nicholson in 1926, is a dense, intimidating text, somewhat like a huge, high mountain rich with deep caves of precious stones and hidden veins of shimmering gold. My exploration and excavations have been enormously enriching and instructive, and I hope these stories will offer the same rewards to the reader.

While growing up in India, I heard Rumi's name in conjunction with other Muslim saints and poets such as Hafiz, Mirza Ghalib, Iqbal, and Kabir. After moving to the United States, I began to see and hear Rumi's name more and more frequently as the years passed. When I moved into Payson Stevens' house, shortly before our marriage, I saw in his library a copy of the three uniquely-colored volumes of the *Mathnawi*. The volumes were part of a larger collection of spiritual books from almost all of the spiritual traditions of the world—bequeathed to Payson by his friend, the photographer, composer, and cellist, Jon Phetteplace, who had died in 1992. I eyeballed the *Mathnawi*. Too much else was happening and I could not afford the luxury of reading such a voluminous work at the time, but I flirted with the idea of one day being able to read it.

However, once I took the books from the shelf, dusted them off, and read the first line of the first volume—*Listen to the reed how it tells a tale, complaining of separation*—I was hooked . . . through the heart. This was Krishna's flute calling to my busy, deaf soul, awakening it, and reminding it of the journey it came here to make. The Sufis call this journey "the Way," and the call was coming to me this time not from the Hindu, but the Islamic Sufi tradition.

That one line created a hunger for more. I read a full page. So much jostled and stirred in such a small space: longing, agony, feeling balanced by thought, thought tempered by emotion, images that opened doorways in the mind and heart. There were no boundaries or distinctions between Rumi's head, heart, and soul: they merged, aiding each other on his journey—as certain as a river in its direction. There was a world here—in a word, in an image. There was a love here that was both physical and transcendent, material and mystical. I knew right away that my relationship as a reader to the *Mathnawi* was not going to be a mere flirtation, but a lifelong marriage.

In 2003, I retold one of Rumi's stories, "The Prison and the Rose Garden," for *Parabola: Tradition, Myth, and the Search for Meaning*. Retelling one story wasn't enough; but at the time, it had to do. I knew that more was in store for me, although I didn't quite know what.

In 2006, after I had finished writing *Ganesha Goes to Lunch*, I knew I wanted to write similar books from all religious traditions. Having been raised as a Sikh, I was taught to believe that all religions are to be respected, be they Christianity, Buddhism, Judaism, etc. The Sikh holy book, *The Granth Sahib*, is a compilation of hymns of Sikh gurus, and Hindu and Sufi saints. Sikh history is rich with Muslim characters. The Sikh gurus believe that all religions are to be revered since they reveal aspects of the same universal truths. My father always strove to remember and practice this belief, giving to individuals in need, no matter what their denominations.

In April 2007, my father died. When I returned to India, where Payson and I live for half the year, I knew I had to begin work on my second book, which would be tales from Rumi. Death is always a call to adventure, and Rumi's three volumes were calling to me. I felt a leap of joy in the midst of my grief. Rumi was my solace all that year and into 2008.

Controversial fragments of biography veil Rumi's beginnings, but most biographers and historians agree upon a few facts: Rumi was born in Persia in the thirteenth century, and lived most of his life in what we now call Turkey. Born into a noble family, he pursued scholarship and jurisprudence. In his late thirties, he met Shams, a ragged, wandering mystic in his sixties. The meeting was transformational for Rumi. The intensity of his relationship with Shams catapulted Rumi into a vision of the universe as experienced through the eyes of love. It plunged Rumi into the wellspring of creativity, and poetry and music began to pour out of him. Shams had kindled in him a love of the divine that was henceforth Rumi's guiding light.

A few years later, when Shams passed away (some say he was murdered by jealous disciples, or perhaps by Rumi's youngest son) Rumi was distraught. When a disciple of Rumi's suggested he write his thoughts into a book, Rumi, it is said, dictated the entire *Mathnawi* over a course of some years. Situated at the interface between the East and West, Rumi was poised to go in both directions. His growing global popularity eight hundred years later is evidence of the abiding relevance of his writing.

Throughout the world, Rumi is known as a Persian poet. Few people know that Rumi is also a master storyteller. He is a Total Being: man, lover, saint, philosopher, poet, metaphysician, jurist, theologian, guide, holy fool, psychologist, and phenomenologist. Rumi is comfortable with and inhabits all of himself.

Perhaps the reason that Rumi is less known for his considerable narrative skills is his meandering style—a style that lends support to the theory that the *Mathnawi* was dictated. Rumi's prose seems better suited to an age less harried than ours, with a different concept of time. To Rumi, whose texts are rich with ruminations on practically all subjects of human interest, time only *appears* to be linear and continuous, but is in fact circular and ever renewing. Rumi's manner of telling his tales, like his concept of time, is also circuitous, tangential, concentric, and eccentric. His stories are habitually interrupted by other stories, long discourses, seeming distractions and digressions, rhapsodies, poetic flights, expositions, and the colloquies and dialectic of a multidimensional soul with itself.

Rumi is very aware of his style, and often even critical of it. A thousand times he berates himself for it: "This discourse hath no end. Go, relate the conclusion of the tale." Or, "This digression has passed beyond bounds." But Rumi's apparent shortcomings are precisely his greatness. We can see in the *Mathnawi* the organic process of a great mind in action. It is clear that if consciousness has a form it is akin to the form of trees and rivers: nonlinear, parallel, and simultaneous—with many branches, tributaries, and distributaries. And his stories, too, reflect this structure.

In his self-awareness as a writer grappling with the material of the human psyche, shapeless thought and feeling, Rumi is very modern. Every writer must encounter the limits of his material, and Rumi confronts his head on. Being a metaphysician, he knows such limits are intimately tied to the limits of language and all its devices: figures of speech, images, symbols, parables, and beyond—to the very nature of all matter and life. Words, images, and metaphors take us only so far on the Way. The transcendent Rumi knows there is a point beyond which his stories cannot go. "The old man has shaken his skirt free from talk and speech. Half of the tale has remained in his mouth," Rumi says at one point. But the artistic Rumi, the storyteller and poet, pushes back the boundaries of the inexpressible again and again, and utilizes his material to perfection. Writing well before Joseph Campbell's treatise on the subject, Rumi makes it very clear that all of his all of his stories (in fact all images and words) are faces—masks to take the writer, and the reader, through the sensory sphere of ordinary human experience to that unseen dimension beyond human thought and conception of which our sensual world and everything in it, including us, is a sign and symbol.

Ultimately, Rumi's works show no division between the secular and the sacred, the literary and the spiritual. The former is a tool in his expert hands for the latter end. The manner and matter of writing becomes the path on which he takes himself, and the reader, to that Ocean of Being into which all empties and from which all returns.

Rumi's stories are a marvelous mix of excellent storytelling and spirituality. Even his bawdy tales carry a spiritual message. In his stories Rumi's social self predominates: the Rumi that is engaged with the drama of relationships—between lovers, husbands and wives, fathers and sons, guides and disciples, humans and God—and above all, the relationship of the human soul with itself. Embedded in the secular lives of humans, these dramatic narratives hold up a mirror and give form to our inner selves, reflecting that amorphous existence we lead beneath the level of conscious thought that determines our reality, the quality of our life, and the extent of our suffering.

Rumi's themes invariably revolve around those human thoughts, desires, cravings, and actions that go against the Cosmic Will. The working of this Will unfolds in the ineluctable and unchangeable Way of the World—what the old world called Destiny, or God's will, or That Which Is. This is at the core of all religions whose main function is to teach humankind how to cope with the inevitable tragedies of life. Islam, the tradition from which Rumi comes, means "submission" and "surrender."

Destiny, an almost forgotten word, is out of fashion these days, but it is central to some of the greatest Western literature, such as the Greek and Shakespearean tragedies. We, in modern times, are inclined to dismiss it as no longer relevant to our technologically driven lives. In our resolve to march forward into a science that we believe will find solutions to all our ills and fix the unfixable, we have buried and left Destiny behind us. We think of it as a prison and cannot see how an acknowledgement of its limits can liberate us to love and joy.

All of Rumi's stories demonstrate the limits of the human will, divorced and at odds with the will of the universe. Most of the characters in these stories persist in ways that create and perpetuate their suffering. They imprison themselves further and further in their attempts to extricate themselves from that which is. Those who learn the imperative lessons of prayer, humility, and surrender, enter the rose garden of paradise. Those who do not, perish, or undergo intense suffering, which is another gateway to the garden.

Sufis have made a cult of suffering, and Rumi emphasizes that all suffering is a gift. Its redemptive purpose is to turn us toward the light and love of that suprasensuous and unseen (though everywhere evident) energy, ubiquitous in and around us, that many call God. "What is Sufism?" someone asks a Sheikh in one of Rumi's stories. The Sheikh replies, "To feel joy in the heart at the coming of sorrow."

The unseen and suprasensuous substratum of all reality, common both to the philosophies, theologies, and experiences of East and West, can only be accessed, Rumi says, in times of loss and tragedy by the eye of the heart: "The water of life is hidden in the land of darkness."

And suffering opens up the heart to love, whether temporal or divine. Physical love is a metaphor for the divine, and trains us for it. As Rumi puts it: "Whether love be earthly or heavenly, in the end it leads us yonder." The Way is love, then, not knowledge. The intellectual search, for Rumi, is far inferior to the spiritual quest. The former is limited and dangerous because it leads to arrogance, pride, blindness, and vainglory while the latter— founded upon love and surrender—leads us to Paradise. Here the veils of our ignorance fall and we are reunited with the source of our being.

Of course, for all enlightened beings, this Paradise is here and now. Our seeming separation from it is a trick of the ego— a shadow cast by our rational minds. For how can anything be separate from the all that is? Such separation is inconceivable and food for wonderment and laughter for the enlightened beings that have become *fana*—who have merged their "i-am-ness" with the "am-ness" of God.

While working on these stories, I have often combined many of Rumi's stories into one—adding names and endings when they were diffuse in the originals, and recreating them for our times. For the purpose of simplification, I have classified the stories in eight sections. The classifications are mine rather than Rumi's, though their themes are ubiquitous in his writings. The narratives primarily demonstrate the themes under which they occur, but on the whole, Rumi's tales are far too complex structurally and metaphysically to be entirely contained within their bounds.

Rumi and his stories are like the delta of a river that splits into many distributaries emptying into the same ocean. The main argument is invariably complemented by many related ideas. A reader new to Rumi would do well not to look with too much focus for a theme, and to understand at the outset a point that Rumi himself belabors throughout the *Mathnawi*: that the story's allegories, analogies, parables, characters, metaphors, symbols, and even words, are devices to clothe, express, and delineate the inexpressible invisible. A lion, a king, or a sultan often stands for God, but not always. It is the context of the story that clarifies the meaning of a metaphor, which cannot be extended too far or taken too literally. In learning to see through the story to its message and meaning, a reader can develop an essential, though always challenging, perception of the Way: to see behind and beyond the senses to the reality reflected in them. "How long," Rumi asks the reader and himself, "will you play at loving the shape of the jug? Leave the shape of the jug, go, go seek the water."

By being thus isolated from Rumi's volumes, these thirty stories both gain and lose. Like a gem worked on by a lapidary and displayed in the bazaars of the world, Rumi is made accessible and his enduring worth and beauty brought before us; but because they have been mined from their matrix, so intimately reflective of Rumi's message of that Whole from which, like the reed from the reed bed, we are separated, I can only hope these stories will lead the serious reader back to the rich and priceless complexity of Rumi's originals. ❀

*Now listen
to the outward form
of a tale, but take heed
to separate the grain
from the chaff.*

RUMI, *MATHNAWI*, BOOK I, 202

# 1

# Surrender to
# God's Will

*It beseems the generous*
*to give money:*
*But the generosity*
*of the lover*
*is surrender*
*of his soul!*

MATHNAWI, I, 2235

◇⊩──◇──⊩◇

*Do not speak, so the Spirit*
*May speak for thee:*
*In the ark of Noah*
*Leave off swimming!*

MATHNAWI, III, 1307

# The Worth of a Pearl

*MATHNAWI, V, 4035-4087*

T SEEMED TO ALL the courtiers that their king, Mahmoud of Ghazni, had gone completely mad. In the morning assembly, he took from his pocket a large, lustrous pearl that filled his hand and glowed even in the day. The king put it in the palm of his vizier, and said to him:

"What do you think is the worth of this pearl?"

"I would guess at least a hundred horse-loads of gold," the vizier replied, rubbing his beard.

"Place the pearl in this mortar and break it with this pestle!" the king commanded him.

"Break it? Your majesty!" the vizier protested. "Surely you are testing me to see whether I am a well-wisher of your treasury! I am, my lord, and will not harm it in any way. This pearl will make your highness far wealthier than you already are, and I wish my king the absolute best in financial matters."

The king was silent a while, and then burst into laughter.

"Well said, well said, old vizier! Here, give me back my pearl, and here is a robe of honor for you as a reward for your loyalty to my treasury!"

After conducting some business of the day, the king once again brought out the pearl from his pocket and put it in the palm of his treasurer, and asked him, "What do you think is the worth of this pearl?"

"At least worth half a kingdom! May God preserve it from destruction and thieves!"

"Break it!" cried the king again, handing him the mortar and pestle.

"Your majesty," the treasurer replied, holding the pearl up to the light. "Never in all my life have I seen anything like it, and I have, as you know, seen many gems. Observe this play of light on its surface, its translucent luster, and its color . . . ah, the best, this shade of delicate rose, which is an indication of its incomparable worth. Observe its roughness to the touch. There can be no doubt this is the real thing. And its shape, ah! A perfect sphere. It comes from at least twenty fathoms deep in the sea and weighs, I would say, about fifteen hundred grains. Ah, your majesty, nothing like this exists in the whole world! Break it? Why, I would sooner break my head!"

The courtiers laughed, and after his customary silence, King Mahmoud joined them in laughter.

"I am surrounded by people who value my treasury! What a boon! I am surrounded by intelligent, practical men bent upon my good." The king said, "Ah, my treasurer, what poetic, descriptive talents you have! How shall I reward you for saving me this wonderful pearl? Here, here's a carriage with six white horses for your very own."

The king wearily conducted some more business, signed some more papers, and discussed plans for another conquest. But once more he returned to the subject of the pearl. This time he put it in the palm of his emir, who had already learned from the example of the others what his response to the king's insane command would be. He, too, waxed poetic over the pearl's worth and beauty, and he, too, was rewarded handsomely for it.

So the king approached all his officials, and all of them preserved the pearl, and all of them received rich rewards and hikes in salary. But by the end of the day, the king looked very dejected and was about to retire for the day when he noticed a rough, ragged looking young man in a torn and patched sheepskin jacket and worn-out shoes standing in the entryway of his court. His lustrous, curly dark hair hung in ringlets about his face, which had a translucent glow upon it like the nacreous shine of the new moon.

"And what's your name?" the king asked.

"Ayaz, Sire," the man bowed low in respect.

"And what do you want, Ayaz?" the king asked.

Ayaz dropped to his knees before the king, held his hand, kissed it, and said, "To love and serve you, Sire!"

"How much do *you* think this pearl is worth?" the king said, dropping the pearl into Ayaz's tough and leathery hand.

"More than I can imagine or say," Ayaz replied.

"Here, put it in this mortar and break it into fragments with this pestle."

Without a moment's thought or doubt, free of anxiety and fear of consequences, oblivious of reward or punishment, Ayaz brought the pestle down with a powerful movement of his hand, and smashed the pearl to a dusty powder.

The people in the court gasped in shock and made a movement to arrest Ayaz.

"You have broken the king's invaluable pearl!" they cried. "Infidel! Uncouth, ignorant fool! Enemy of the king! Kill him! Kill him!"

The king's many ministers pounced on Ayaz and would have finished him off if the king hadn't intervened.

"Release him!" cried King Mahmoud.

The officers reluctantly let him go. The poor shepherd looked even more ragged and disheveled in his doubly torn sheepskin jacket.

"What do you have to say for yourself, young man?" the king queried.

"Princes, renowned officials," Ayaz said. "Is the king's command more precious—or a pearl? Your gaze is fixed upon the pearl, not upon the king. Compared to his command this pearl is just a colored stone."

The king's eyes lit up with joy and all his exhaustion fell from him. He walked over to Ayaz, and his dirty outfit not withstanding, held him near his heart, and whispered, "Here is my heart, my Ayaz, my pearl, my treasure. I have found you!" ֍

# And This Belongs To ...

*MATHNAWI, I, 3013-3123*

 CLEVER OLD WOLF was always hungry. There simply wasn't enough prey in the jungle in which he lived, and though the mountains above were teeming with food, the many lions there were a threat to his life. So he came up with a strategy to satisfy his hunger. He would go and make an alliance with the head lion, King of the Wilderness. He would also enlist the aid of his neighbor, the fox. United, they would go on a hunt to the dangerous mountains where there was plenty of prey. Their combined efforts would ensure success.

The wolf went to his neighbor, the thin and straggly fox who had a mate and many offspring. The little ones were trying to play, but were exhausted from hunger, so they lay about looking sad and thin. The wolf explained his plan to the fox, and added, "You'll have plenty of fresh, warm meat for yourself and your family! Come, join me in this venture!" The hungry fox was easily convinced and became his ally.

Together the wolf and the fox approached the majestic and grand lion who lay outside his lair, taking a snooze in the sun.

"O king of the jungle and of the mountains, we have come to you with a plan," the wolf said.

The lion heard them out, got up, roared, and stretched. He didn't need the wolf and the fox to accompany him on his hunts, but he decided to honor the two with his company so their hungers could be satisfied.

Up in the mountains they had no trouble finding prey. The fox hounded out the animals with his sense of smell, the wolf circled and trapped them, and the lion killed them easily. Together they bought down a mountain ox, a fat boar, and a wild goat.

As they dragged the dead animals down the mountainside, the hungry wolf and the fox each wondered if the lion would share the spoils of the hunt with them. They feared the lion would eat the kill all by himself and not leave anything for them. Hadn't they participated in the hunt? Would the lion have succeeded without their help? Their fears alternated with hope that the lion would be just, and divide the meat fairly amongst them.

They piled their booty in the center of a clearing in the forest, and the lion said to the wolf, "O wolf, be my assistant and divide this prey amongst the three of us. And be just."

"What could be easier?" thought the wolf to himself. Aloud, he said, "O big and strong king, the large and hefty mountain ox is yours; the boar is mine, and the goat belongs to the fox."

Having said this, the wolf, who had no doubt in his mind that he had done the fair and just thing, stood proudly aside. The fox, too, was very pleased with this judgment, though he didn't show it.

"Is that your final decision?" The lion asked.

"Yes, your majesty," the wolf replied, bowing before him.

"When I am here," the lion roared, his voice resounding through the forest, "how can you speak of 'I' and 'you?'" Then the lion pounced on the wolf and tore him to bits with his fierce claws.

The fox shivered inside his fur as he watched in horror while his neighbor was shredded to pieces before his eyes.

"You, fox, go ahead now, and divide this prey for our breakfast."

The fox had a moment of terror, and then a flash of insight flared in his brain. He bowed low before the lion, and said, "This fat ox will be your breakfast, O wonderful king! And this juicy boar will be . . . your lunch. And this plump goat shall be . . . yours, O bountiful king, for supper."

"And what about you?" the lion asked.

"Everything is yours, O King! You alone have made this abundance possible. Without you, none of this would have come to be. It is only in your mercy that all the creatures of this forest live and flourish. I am but a small part of you, and entirely yours. What you give me I shall eat, and what you withhold, too, shall be a gift."

"Who taught you your wisdom, O fox?"

"You did O glorious king, and . . . the fate of my unfortunate neighbor, the wolf."

"Ah, then take all three animals, for they are yours. Since you have become entirely mine, I am you and you are me. How then can I hurt or deprive you of anything?"

The lion turned around and walked away to his lair. The fox thought to himself, "A hundred thousand thanks to the lion for asking the wolf first to make the division. If he had asked me first, how would I have escaped with my life, and all this bounty? How fortunate we are to come into this world after those who have gone before us, so we can take warning from their fate."

# The Witch of Kabul

MATHNAWI, IV, 3085-3188; VI, 1222-1292

ING KAFUR OF KABUL was given to musing and introspection on the state of his soul and the world. Every event, every dream, every thought and emotion became fodder for reflection and wonder.

One night he dreamt that his son, the prince Tawfiq, the light of his life, died suddenly. The king's grief was so intense that, in dream, he himself was brought to the very verge of death. In the convulsion of his death throes he awoke with a start. Realizing his son had only died in a dream, the king was filled with an unbounded joy so powerful that he felt he was dying from it. When he recovered sufficiently from the grip of these powerful passions, King Kafur laughed aloud at the folly of man destined to live thus in the troughs and crests of contrary emotions. As he walked in his beautiful garden full of rare flowers, exotic trees, and songbirds, he mused about how easy it was for blind humanity to drown in the illusions of the world.

But King Kafur's dream had taught him something: life was uncertain and perishable. Because the king had not yet learnt the lesson that when the candle of the body begins to perish, one needs to light the candle of the spirit, he resolved to light another lamp from the lamp of his mortal son: marry him so he could beget a son. To this end he began to search his kingdom for a suitable bride.

Meanwhile, in another strand of the story, there lived in Kabul a ninety-year-old hag called Aliya who had never married. She hadn't wanted or needed to. Having been youthful late into her life, and beautiful, too, she had had her pick of lovers. But at the age of ninety, when no one would have her, she was extremely lonely and craved to have a man around her permanently. She longed to have a glamorous wedding. Though her body was falling apart, her heart was young, and her passions still raged. Oh, to dress up as a bride! To wait for her beloved to come to her on the wedding night on the bed strewn with jasmines and rose petals! Oh, to be naked, skin to burning skin, with her lover!

Aliya resolved to fulfill her dreams by whatever means possible before she died.

She began first by trying to repair her decrepit body. She went to surgeons to get her sagging breasts uplifted; she applied salves and unguents to her skin, which was wrinkled like the neck of an old camel; dyes to her hair that had turned white like muddied snow; oils to her bare gums to make her teeth grow back. She got massages to straighten her back, which was bent like a bow; plucked her eyebrows; applied rouge to her cheeks and kohl to her eyes. But all her efforts made her look more haggard, like a dilapidated house whose walls and ceiling had caved, but whose door was painted in loud and garish colors.

When all Aliya's efforts failed, the old crone, who had no spiritual leanings, tried another trick. She had heard about the power of the Koran, but instead of reading it and contemplating its wisdom, she cut off portions of the Holy Book and stuck them to her face to hide the creases and crevices. But whenever she moved or put on her *chador*, the bits of paper fell off. She put spittle on them and stuck them to her face again. But when she spoke or chewed, they fell off again. She glued them on with firmer glue, and went before the object of her passions, which happened to be Prince Tawfiq, and laughed coyly.

Tawfiq, a good Sufi who lived for the now and paid no heed to tomorrow, on guard against the thousand distractions that way lay humans from moment to moment, saw through Aliya's depraved intentions, spurred his horse whenever he saw her on the street and galloped past her as fast as he could.

Frustrated beyond measure, Aliya called on Iblis (Satan), to give her beauty, youth, and wealth with which to ensnare the object of her craving.

"Leave me alone, you foul hag!" Iblis spat as soon as she evoked him.

"Help me!" she screamed.

She was so repulsive that even Iblis began to wax spiritual.

"Scrape off your lusts from the mirror of your heart, you old harlot, and make your cleansed heart your beauty."

But Aliya was persistent in her pleadings. Iblis, who was incapable of bestowing either beauty or youth, was eager to rid himself of her. He gave her a vial of glittering dust that would give her the illusion of youth, beauty, and wealth if she sprinkled it on whomever she wanted to enchant. The dust would only work on a person who had momentarily lapsed in his vigilance against the sorcery of the world.

King Kafur, meanwhile, began his search for a bride for Tawfiq. He resolved to find a girl who was poor, but beautiful and virtuous, rather than a haughty and wealthy princess. He found such a girl in a distant corner of his kingdom. Fauzia was the daughter of an ascetic, and her beauty and virtue were inexpressible in words. Let it be sufficient to say that she was a union of all that is best and highest in human nature, steady and unwavering on her path to abide by what is true beneath all the glitter and falsity of the world.

Riding his horse on the way to his wedding, the prince passed by Aliya in the narrow streets. Preoccupied by thoughts of his ensuing wedding, he was not paying as much attention as usual. Aliya sprinkled her glittering dust on him, and instantly, the prince reigned in his horse. Charmed by Aliya's coy laughter, he took one look into the sunken, puffy eyes in her haggard face, which was plastered over with fragments of the Koran, and was smitten beyond remedy. Like a spider, she had caught him in her web and tightened her knots around his heart.

Prince Tawfiq got off his horse and followed the old crone. The world glittered and shimmered all around him. The narrow, dirty streets became winding garden paths, the crumbling houses became palaces, the ankle bells on Aliya's feet as she walked ahead of him were the most enticing of sounds, her cracked and crumbling heels were the most alluring of bodily parts, and the folds of her filthy chador were the diaphanous veils of a mystery that held the deepest of sensual pleasures.

King Kafur and Fauzia waited and waited at the wedding, but Tawfiq did not come. Although Fauzia did not despair or give up hope, when King Kafur heard what had happened to his son, he was distraught. As if in mourning with the king, all the vegetation in his kingdom and in his garden began to wither and die. Even the songbirds became silent. The king sent many anguished messages to his son to open his eyes to the truth of his enchantment, but the prince was deaf to them all. Tawfiq was not capable of extricating himself from the clutches of the witch, nor did he feel the need to. He was in bliss, bestowing kisses on the soles of the hag's shoes, and staring into her eyes for hours on end. His father was just a doddering old fool with his spiritual mumbo-jumbo, the prince thought. Life was for living, and sitting at the feet of his beautiful, dark goddess. Yes, he was probably trapped, like his father said he was, but what a sweet trap Aliya was! He was not in her "clutches," as his father called it, but in her scintillating embrace.

An entire year passed, in which Tawfiq's wife-to-be waited patiently, with unwavering hope for her beloved. King Kafur despaired for himself and his son, and forgot altogether to muse and contemplate with detachment the state of the human being so prone to delusion and despair. He wanted so much for his son to return to the Way that his seduction out of it by the old hag caused him immeasurable anguish.

Once more, as in his dream, King Kafur found himself standing before the door of death. With one foot already in the door, he awoke suddenly to the realization that instead of judging his son for being in the clutches of the witch, he should have judged himself for being in the clutches of his own despair! He was just as deluded as his son.

He sat down, turned his attention towards the dark labyrinths of his own heart, traveled through them to the abode of his Beloved, God, and surrendered himself and his son to the mystery of life and its entrapments.

"You alone, O God, have commanded this to happen. How could anything in the world be without your will?"

King Kafur gave up all attempts to force his son back to the Path, surrendered his own will and wanting to the will of God, and henceforth stayed with soft supplications and prayers.

King Kafur looked up and saw in the distance undulating waves of light coming towards him. As they got nearer, a radiant figure emerged from it. The king knew help had arrived from the land of the Invisible. It was a master magician who alone could engage in combat with Iblis's forces on earth, and with Aliya, the crone.

How the master magician defeated Aliya after a protracted battle in the tombs of Kabul by using the same delusions as hers is another long story. Suffice it to say Aliya was defeated, and the gnarled knots she had bound around the prince's heart were released.

The prince's eyes opened, and as he looked at Aliya, shorn of all her magic, standing before him with her little bits of paper stuck all over her crumbling face, he was amazed at his bewitchment. He began to be repulsed at himself, but caught himself and surrendered his impurity to God, who makes all things pure. He felt the stirring of a deep compassion in his heart for this crumpled up old woman who did not know when to turn away from the things of the world towards another beauty and another love that was imperishable and ever renewing.

"I have to go now," he said, looking at her in a way nobody else had ever looked at her before. There was such kindness in that look that Aliya felt affirmed and loved for who she was beneath all her appearance. Though her heart was full of suffering and sorrow, she knew that in time she would be able to endure the truth about the state of her body and its unending desire, surrender to the will of God who has made everything perishable, and turn towards a love that could only grow with time, a love that would make her younger by the day even as her body disintegrated further into dust.

Then Prince Tawfiq turned from her and went back to his father, a sword in one hand and a shroud in another. He fell at his father's feet.

"Kill me father, for I have erred," he wept. "I deserve no less."

The king lifted him up, and embraced him. "I too have erred, son," he said, wiping his own and his son's tears.

"I was bewitched by the witch of Kabul," the prince said.

"The world is the witch of Kabul, my son. It is our difficult task to always tread the path of Truth. Come, your bride awaits you."

And as the prince rode his horse towards his true wife's abode, all the bare trees blossomed and the birds began to sing. 🌸

# 11

# Embrace
# Suffering

*The Friend is like gold,*
*tribulation is like the fire:*
*the pure gold is glad*
*in the heart of fire.*

MATHNAWI, II, BOOK II, 1461

◊⊩—◊—⊩◊

*When the blossom is shed,*
*the fruit comes to a head;*
*when the body is shattered,*
*the spirit lifts up its head.*

MATHNAWI, I, 2929

# You Never Know Why

MATHNAWI, II, 1878-1912

 HMED WAS SLEEPING peacefully in an orchard when he was suddenly and rudely awakened to find that, for no reason, a stranger was beating him to a pulp.

"What . . .? Why are you . . .?" Ahmed asked, but only more blows answered his queries. The stranger's eyes bulged with rage, and he refused to talk.

Stunned, barely awake, and wondering if he was having a nightmare, Ahmed tried to ward off the blows with his hands, but the onslaught was relentless.

"O God," Ahmed cried inwardly. "What sin have I committed? I am a good man, and I haven't harmed anyone. Why then are you punishing me?"

Ahmed managed to run away from the stranger as fast as he could, and rested, panting and frothing, under an apple tree. But the crazy stranger pursued him, and grabbed him under the tree.

"Who are you and what have I done to you . . .?" Ahmed began, but the stranger was obviously deranged. At the point of his sword, he forced Ahmed to eat the rotten apples that had fallen on the ground.

"But why . . .?"

"Eat! Eat! Faster! More!" cried the stranger, stuffing the apples into Ahmed's mouth.

Ahmed had many questions to ask the stranger, but his mouth was full of apples. Nonplussed and almost crazed with the situation, Ahmed replayed in his mind all the other tragedies that had befallen him in his life, and came to the conclusion that life was inherently absurd and full of meaningless suffering like the kind he was undergoing right then.

"I curse you!" Ahmed screamed inwardly at the stranger. His stomach was so full that he couldn't breathe. And just when he thought he was going to pass out, the stranger took out a whip and began to beat him with it.

"Run," screamed the stranger. "Run! Faster! Faster!" Gorged with the apples, exhausted, sleepy, his feet and face covered with bleeding sores and wounds, Ahmed ran and ran, the stranger in hot pursuit. All night the stranger chased and tortured him. At dawn they came to a stream, and the stranger made Ahmed go down on his knees and drink the water like an animal.

"Drink!" he yelled. "More, drink more!"

Ahmed drank till he could drink no more, then sat up on the bank, and threw up everything he had eaten and drunk.

"This is the end," he thought to himself. "We suffer like this all our lives and then we die."

He looked up at the stranger and said, "I will die easily if you just tell me why."

Without any words, the stranger pointed with his sword at Ahmed's vomit. There, amidst the rotten apples lay a long, black snake, writhing and hissing, his tongue darting in and out of his mouth.

"I was riding by when I saw the snake slither into your open, snoring mouth," the stranger explained.

"But . . . but why didn't you just tell me the reason? I would have obeyed you meekly, done everything you asked me to, and borne your blows knowing that my suffering had a purpose!"

"Because," replied the stranger, sheathing his sword and

putting away his mace and whip, "had I told you that you had swallowed a black snake, you would have died of fright. This was the lesser suffering."

Ahmed fell at the feet of the stranger, and said, "O blessed is the hour you saw me. Blessed is the suffering you inflicted to awaken me." ⚘

# Pilgrimage to Paradise

*MATHNAWI*, I, 1913-2222

N THE TIME OF OMAR, the second Caliph of Islam, there lived in Medina a man called Tasleem. He was a harpist with such a beautiful, versatile voice—which ranged from bass to treble with equal ease—that it made elephants grow wings, nightingales shameful of their song, and the dead quicken in their winding sheets and sit up in amazement and joy. He was courted, wined, and dined by high and low. Wherever he went, cheering crowds followed him, bowing and clapping in admiration and adulation.

As time passed, Tasleem's lungs lost their power, his vocal chords their control, his voice its beauty, and his fingers their agility. As he aged, the voice that was once the envy and joy of all became like the braying of an old donkey. He awoke on his seventieth birthday to find that his audience had abandoned him for newer, fresher talent. Since Tasleem—confident in the enduring nature of his popularity—had spent his huge fortune on frivolous things, he was now in debt, his landlord had thrown him out for delinquency, the inspectors were chasing him for unpaid taxes, and he didn't have money to buy even a loaf of bread. And what was worse, he couldn't afford strings for his harp.

Amazed at the turn of events in his life, and desperate, Tasleem stumbled out of his home, his unstrung harp in his arms, and a bitter monologue in his head. How could Allah, if He was kind, as people said He was, make him suffer like this? People had called Tasleem God's minstrel, and Tasleem knew it to be true. But did He not care for his own minstrel? Did He not blink an eye at the decay of a talent such as his? Was there any justice in His world?

As Tasleem walked the streets, no one paid the slightest attention to him. He looked at their faces to see if they recognized him. A few did, but after a brief *salaam*, passed him by. They were all hurrying to hear their favorite minstrel, a man less accomplished and versatile with the harp and his voice, but younger and more passionate than Tasleem. Despondent and desperate, Tasleem walked aimlessly, uncertain of his direction, not knowing where to go. His heart and his world were in ruins.

Tasleem's footsteps led him to the graveyard outside Medina. Hungry and weary, he sat down on a tomb. What, he wondered, had his life meant? The world that had bestowed such honors on him was a lie. Even the fame of his youth, so heady at the time, was now only a bitter memory. He would never be able to play his harp and sing; and the inability to sing was a living hell. Or even if he could croak a little, it would only be poison in contrast to his earlier ability. No, all was lost. Suffering and desperation alone remained.

Perhaps, Tasleem thought, the sins of his youth, his pride in his talent and his fame, had caught up with him, and he was being punished. Looking at the graves around him, Tasleem felt some comfort: at least his sorrow had an end.

"I suppose," Tasleem thought, "I should say a prayer before I die. Death is a big event, and I am a bit afraid of it." Tasleem shut his eyes and didn't know where to begin. He had never really prayed before. He had lived long stretches of time without even thinking of Allah. He hadn't needed to. Wasn't fame and fortune what most people prayed for, anyway? They had come to him without his asking, seeking, or striving. He had felt like a chosen one, special, the favorite of fortune, a child of the universe. But now, suddenly, here he was, a tiny coagulum of matter and mind that had arisen like a bubble from the ocean of being, on the verge of dissolution back into it. Oblivion. He would become food for worms in the airless chamber of earth's darkness.

The minstrel stretched out on the tomb, conscious of the dirt and bones beneath him, which had once belonged to a suffering person. He had never paid much thought to suffering. It was always something others felt. Although some suffering had touched him now and then (ubiquitous as air, how could it not?), song had always mitigated it: song was his wings, his life, his bread, his drink, his breath, and his joy.

"Allah . . ." he began, and suddenly a sob arose in his heart, dissolving the knot of doubt and anguish in his heart. "You have taken away my song, which was my breath and my bread. How can I live without it? It's true; you have bestowed many favors on this old wretch. You have given me a long life and, even though I no longer have it, success beyond my imagining. You, who have given me everything without my asking, have taken away from me all that you have given. Take it. It was always yours. Help me to embrace this suffering that you have visited upon me. I am naked and helpless at your door. Make me your guest. If I live, I am yours alone, and I will play my harp only for you. But please send me enough money for harp strings—for you, in your mercy, forgive even those that err and forget you."

Then the minstrel sang a few refrains in a voice wracked by tears, and making his harp his pillow, lay down on a grave. The bird of his soul escaped from the prison of his existence, and flew away, leaving harp and harpist behind.

Without head or foot, without feathers or wings, Tasleem's soul journeyed beyond the realm of time to the unconfined spaces of a garden with mystic, unfading flowers, anemones and roses, jasmines and orchids. Here, without hands, it gathered bouquets of undying flowers. Without eyes or light, it perceived worlds. Without a body, it sat by Salsabil, the fountain of the heart, and sang, without lips and tongue, throat and lungs, harp and strings, songs of its previous, dream-like life, and all that had befallen it while it was imprisoned in the cage of the body. Having experienced *this*, it could never again be content with *that*—the sensual, material, conflicted world of contraries. Tasleem's soul was plunged in a sea of honey in which it bathed and was purged of its afflictions, and made pure like a sunrise. Yes, it was happy and content here, far, far beyond the satisfaction of fame, fortune, and even, yes, even of his joy in song. *I* and *me* and *mine* dissolved in a greater unity and identity that his soul—still trying to formulate its experience, still tied to words and description—could only call . . . *Thou.*

Ah, it had arrived home. It never wanted to leave.

No sooner than it had this thought than the voice, the original vibration that created all matter and of which all other sounds are but echoes, came to its earless ear:

"Don't get attached to this and tarry here. It is just another experience. Depart now!"

"What?" it thought. "Return to *that*? No, no, not yet."

Meanwhile, in *that* world, Omar, the Caliph, benevolent ruler, man of God, philosopher king, sitting in his hall of judgment, suddenly felt a great drowsiness come upon him. He was amazed at it, but saying to himself, "What a mystery this sudden sleepiness is! It is sent to me from the Unseen, and must have a purpose." He allowed himself to fall into a deep slumber.

In his dream, Omar heard the voice of that original vibration, simultaneous, eternal, everywhere at once: "O Omar, take seven hundred dinars from your treasury and give them to my favorite servant, a chosen one, pure and blessed and worthy, who is even now in the graveyard of Medina. Tell him to buy strings for his harp."

Omar awoke, put money in a pouch, and rushed off to the graveyard. He ran from grave to grave but no one was there, just a decrepit old man sleeping on a tomb. Omar exhausted himself looking for a man who looked pure and blessed, but found none but the decrepit old man. How could such a ragged-looking person be the chosen of God? And when all his efforts failed to find another, Omar realized, again, how deluded he was in judging by appearances.

"What a fool I am!" Omar thought. "How unable I am to learn the truth once and for all! But like a child I always forget and relearn, endlessly."

Omar walked over to the sleeping man and sat beside him, reverently and silently waiting for the minstrel, whom he now recognized through his rags, to awaken. And as Omar sat there, something tickled his nose. . . .

Gamboling in the waters of Salsabil, Tasleem heard a loud sound.

"A . . a . . .a . . . ch. . . ch. . . .choo . . . . ooo . . . .!"

Omar's loud sneeze acted as an urgent summons to the minstrel's soul. It didn't want to leave, but from its pilgrimage to paradise it had learned that even a sneeze had a purpose. So it surrendered to the call, and descended down the gossamer, silver strands that tied him to his comatose body lying upon the grave, in the world of form and color, money and debt, taxes and rent, praise and blame. It slipped into its body like a foot into a shoe.

Startled and upset, Tasleem sat up on the tomb and looked at the man sitting next to him. The minstrel sprang to his feet, and fell at the feet of the man.

"Oh, for Allah's sake," he cried, "do not imprison me for my debts! I beg you, sir; kindly let me off this time."

"Do not fear," Omar hastened to reply in a reassuring, gentle voice. "I bring good tidings. Here are seven hundred dinars. Spend them on whatever you need, and of course, buy harp strings."

This unusual event did not seem too strange to Tasleem, who had experienced far stranger things. He extended his hand and accepted the money. Staring at it, he was overcome by remorse and shame. He handed the money back to Omar, then in a distracted state broke his harp against the tomb, and began to tear off his garments.

"Why are you doing this? You are the chosen of God, and very dear to Him. He it was who . . ."

"Stop! Stop!" cried the minstrel. "I am unworthy! I curse this harp that separated me from Him! I curse my voice that led me away by its beauty! I curse my ambition that cast a veil between Him and me. Oh, I have wasted my life away in treble and bass, in musical modes, in rhythms, and melodies. While I was busy being famous, the caravan passed me by and the day grew late. I have frittered away my youth in garnering praise! Oh, I have been so full of sin, so stuffed with ego that I paid no attention to Him who is dearer to me than this false and deluding 'I.'"

"Oh, do stop this wailing and whining," Omar said. "It is also created by your ego. *Was, is, will be* are curtains that separate you from Him. Don't you see how you are vacillating between the low treble of despair to the high sound of this weeping? Control yourself! Your repentance only prolongs your sin."

"But the harp has been my problem. I should give it up, retire, and go seek the treasure that is God."

"The harp, O minstrel, is God's gift to you. Why else would he bid me bring you this money for your harp stings? And how does earning a livelihood prevent the discovery of treasure? Do not retire from work. God sings through your song."

Tasleem looked at Omar and an exchange happened between their eyes that initiated the minstrel into the mystery of mysteries. The minstrel became suddenly still, beyond weeping and laughter. He was absorbed into the oneness beyond all duality. The world of form and color became contiguous with the Invisible.

He took the money from Omar, bowed to him, thanked him for awakening his heart, and returned to the bazaars to buy himself a new harp and strings. He would play and sing now for God, instead of an audience that praised and censured, rewarded and punished.

The minstrel went into seclusion and played the melodies that no ear has ever heard. He entered that state of silence and repose where this story, tethered to words, cannot follow. ✿

# The Gift

MATHNAWI, I, 3157-3215

ARK HADN'T SEEN Joseph, a childhood friend from Canaan, for many, many years. They had played together, grazed sheep together, and lain under the stars and shared their dreams together. Mark had loved Joseph deeply, though his mind often got in the way of his devotion. Mark had questioned Joseph's faith in a divine plan for the universe and for humans, and doubted his friend's simple and grand convictions.

"See this coat of many colors?" Joseph had once said to him as they lay in the shade of a tree. "It is thus with our experiences, Mark. The light and dark colors blend into and emerge out of each other, seamlessly. You cannot remove one pattern or color without destroying the whole."

Mark had sought out Joseph whenever he could, for in his company and presence the universe, which he often thought to be a malignant force, became beneficent and kind, and the face of his friend made his soul dance.

Then one day Joseph suddenly disappeared, and it was rumored that a wild animal had killed him as he and his brothers had gone to feed their father's flock of sheep. Joseph's brothers had brought back his bloodstained coat of many colors as evidence of his death.

Stunned and sorrowful, Mark had mourned his friend for a long time. His mourning, however, was colored with many doubts. He had been familiar with Joseph's brothers' jealousy of their younger sibling. Mark felt certain his brothers had done Joseph harm. Embittered, Mark roamed the world aimlessly, traveling from one place to another, but wherever he went, he could not escape from the prison of his beliefs. He deeply doubted that a universe that destroyed a person as noble as Joseph, at such a young age, could have any pattern or meaning.

Then one day while he was in Turkey, a traveler from Egypt told Mark that Joseph, son of Jacob, from Canaan, was alive! And not only alive, but was governor of all of Egypt! Mark's heart had somersaulted madly at the news, and as he heard the tale from the traveler, flares of hope, like the light of stars in the black cloth of night, flickered and danced in his soul. Was it possible? Dare he hope to see his friend again? And . . . Oh joy . . . could Joseph's vision of the universe still be the right one, after all?

As the days passed, Mark became more and more hopeful of meeting with his beloved friend. One day in the bazaars of Turkey, he saw a shop full of beautiful things and recalled a time when, as youths, they had been sitting on boulders by a stream and Joseph had been talking about the necessity of keeping faith in the promise of being God's guest some day, of dining with Him in His bounty.

"If you do not have this faith," Joseph had said, "then from His kitchen you will get only dust and ashes. So prepare, prepare, prepare for the Meeting, my friend!" Joseph had said with eyes burning with passion.

"And how should one prepare?" Mark had asked, perplexed at Joseph's meaning.

"Sleep and eat little. Stir a little, like the embryo, so you may be given the senses that behold the Light of the Unseen world. And when you emerge from this womb-like earth into the vast expanse, into which the saints have entered, and go to the court of the Friend, go not empty handed, but take the gift of this stirring."

Mark had not understood Joseph, who often spoke, it seemed to him, in obscure riddles.

But the memory reminded Mark to buy a gift for his friend, who he was now hopeful of meeting.

He spent a long time searching for the right gift, knowing that whatever he bought for Joseph would be paltry for the governor of Egypt. After much thought and many deliberations, Mark bought a gift with his savings. Turning toward Egypt, his heart soared on the crests of hope and plunged into the troughs of despair: would Joseph even remember him?

But when he finally reached Joseph's door, it opened immediately, and there, instead of a servant, as Mark had expected, stood Joseph himself, his arms wide open. Mark walked into them and sobbed, while Joseph held him near his heart.

Later, Mark fed from Joseph's table, laden with an abundance of fruit and other food. Afterwards, they lay upon cushions and reminisced about the old days. Joseph told Mark his story: how, in their jealousy of him, his brothers had stripped him of his coat and thrown him into a well; how they had later taken him out and sold him for twenty pieces of silver to the Ishmaelites, who sold him to Potiphar, Pharaoh's captain of the guard. He told how Potiphar had made him the head of his household, and how later he was sent to prison because Potiphar's wife had falsely accused Joseph of trying to seduce her. He explained how his skill of interpreting dreams had released him and he had gone to Pharaoh's court and was made governor of all the lands; how a famine in Canaan had brought his brothers to Egypt for corn; how they had met, and how Joseph had forgiven them.

"Forgiven them?" Mark, who had been seething with rage at Joseph's brothers, leapt up from the cushion and said. "How could you forgive them? They threw you into a well! You could have died in it! How could you forgive those who threw you into the furnace of suffering?"

"Like the moon. When she is waning, she knows she will be full again."

"I don't understand!" Mark broke out. "You could have been buried alive in the bowels of the earth! And it was because of them you ended up in prison!"

"When a seed of corn is buried in the earth, Mark, my friend," said Joseph, putting his arm around Mark's shoulders, "it rises up as an ear of corn. When the corn is crushed in the mill, its value increases and it becomes bread. When the bread is crushed under our teeth, it becomes the mind and spirit. When does anything ever decrease by suffering and dying?"

A mote of understanding glimmered in Mark's mind. He wanted to bow down before Joseph and kiss his feet, but held himself back. His love for his friend left no room for doubt. Joseph knew how to make affliction yield fruit and was far, far above Mark's own spiritual state. The way for him to live now was in the reflection of his friend, and try in whatever way he could to emulate his ways. But how? Did he have it in him, or was he doomed forever to flounder on the Way?

"God," said Joseph, divining Mark's thoughts, "causes all to happen."

There was a long pause. Then Joseph said, "Now, Mark, tell me, what gift have you brought for me?"

"I couldn't think of anything worthy enough of you! How could I bring a grain of gold to a mine? How could I bring a drop of water to the sea?"

"But come, come, show me what you brought."

"I couldn't bring anything that you don't already have, and . . ."

"Let me see it!" Joseph said, playfully reaching into Mark's bag, while the latter shamefully held on to it. After a joyful tussle, Joseph gained control.

"A mirror!" Joseph exclaimed. "And what a beautiful mirror!"

"I bought it . . . because you are so beautiful . . . and because you reflect the possibility for mankind . . . and . . ." Mark embarrassedly tried to explain his choice of the gift.

"Come, my friend, come. Tell me, why did you really buy this?" Joseph teased.

"Because," said Mark, bursting into tears. "When I see myself in a mirror, I see only defects. And I hope . . . and pray that I become empty as a mirror, so that whenever you look into it, I will reflect you. With this mirror keep a little bit of me around you forever!" Mark said, falling at Joseph's feet and kissing them.

"I will do better than that," Joseph said, picking him up and holding him. "I will keep *you* in my heart forever, my Mark!" ☙

# Taming the Tiger

MATHNAWI, VI, 3044-2138

DERVISH BRAVED A LONG and arduous journey through scorching desert and frightening forest, up steep mountains and down dangerous gorges to visit Sheikh Abu Hasan of whose saintliness he had heard a great deal. The dervish wanted to be his disciple, and to learn from him how to be a saintly person.

Though his suffering on his quest was considerable, nothing compared to what he faced when he knocked on the Sheikh's door.

"What do you want?" said the Sheikh's wife, opening the door with a rolling pin in her hand and patches of white flour on her scowling, growling face. Loose wisps of white hair escaped from under her black headscarf above eyes blazing with hostility.

"Kind woman . . ." the dervish began, hoping the rolling pin meant some bread at least.

"Skip the compliments. Ask your business and be on your way," she barked.

"I have traveled long and hard to get one small glimpse of the holy saint, Sheikh Abu Hasan. . . ."

"Holy!" cried the woman, her face contorted into a snarl. "Holy! That scoundrel who deludes everyone into worshiping his holiness! Saint! This weak and miserable man, a saint! Don't you have better things to do? You could have spared yourself a lot of trouble. Now be on your way and stop wasting my time!"

"Please!" the dervish said before she could shut the door on his face. "I have come a long way. I wish to meet him."

"Why do you want to meet that imposter and parasite? While I cook and clean and mend, he is busy spouting philosophy and loudly beating his own drum. His words are hollow, his wisdom a sham!"

"The man you call an imposter and parasite is a shining light, woman!"

"You must have hair growing out of your eyeballs, stupid man, to see this shining light. Shining light, indeed, like the bottom of my skillet!"

"His splendor has reached East and West and you don't know it?"

"East and West! Is that how far the sound of his drum has reached? He deserves a knock on his head, like this, that will show him the stars!" Abu Hasan's wife hit the dervish on the head with her rolling pin.

The dervish lunged at her, feeling a primitive, animal energy surging within him. He felt the urge to tear her to pieces with his bare hands, but remembering who she was, controlled himself. He couldn't restrain himself from cursing her verbally, however.

"You blithering old hag! You should be grateful to be a dog in his house!"

Hasan's wife screwed up her face and spat at the dervish.

"I spit at you and spit at him!" she hissed.

"If you weren't his wife, I would tear you to pieces, you . . . devil!" roared the dervish. "May your lips and mouth and throat rot for spitting at the moon and the sky! What a disgrace, a man like him married to a rotten, maggot-infested corpse like you!"

The woman hit him again with the rolling pin, and then slammed the door on his face.

"I'm not a cloud that you can chase me away so easily, you beast! Your husband . . . ugh, it makes me want to vomit that he's paired with you! An angel of God, married to the devil! But you won't make me turn back from him," the dervish screamed. "Don't think your ugliness will keep me from seeking him till the end of my days!"

"Seek him in hell!" screamed the wife from inside.

Fuming with rage, the dervish threw himself at the door, which was locked firmly from the inside. He turned away, terribly agitated, and confused and upset at his agitation. He sat outside the door for a while, his head clasped in his hands, his heart in turmoil at his own violent inclinations. Had he been wrong about the Sheikh? Was his arduous journey wasted? If the Sheikh were really as enlightened as they said he was, would he be married to such a devil of a harridan? Perhaps the Sheikh was married to her only out of lust. The dervish could see how she must once have been a beautiful, young woman. Had he failed in his quest? Should he just go home?

But the dervish was not willing to turn back just yet. He finally found a kind woman in the village that fed him and told him the Sheikh had gone to the hills nearby to collect firewood. The dervish went to the forest, his heart, like straw, aflame with doubt and smoking as it burned.

The dervish, so lost in his thoughts and perplexity, suddenly became aware of a loud growling close by. Suddenly, a large, powerful tiger burst out of the underbrush and leaped on him. The dervish tumbled into the thorny bushes in fear and heard a voice above him say in a gentle, sweet voice, "Easy, easy. Leave him alone. He has come to meet me."

The dervish opened his eyes and found himself staring into the wide-open, red jaws of a fierce tiger carrying wood on his back. Upon the sticks sat a turbaned man with a flowing, white beard. In his hand was a long black whip, which moved and writhed with a life of its own. The dervish looked closer and saw it was a serpent.

The dervish sat up and looked at Abu Hasan in astonishment. A soft, warm, tender light played about his glowing face and beard. Had his search for the saint brought him to a strange, mystic, magical, mythic world where the impossible was true, the dervish wondered, or was he just dreaming?

"So, you've met her?" Abu Hasan laughed. "And she has filled you with rage, smoke, and doubt? Don't be tempted by the tigers of your doubt, my friend. Ride them."

"But how can such an injustice . . . such disharmony . . . so much . . . filth . . ." the dervish sputtered, unable to formulate his bewilderment at this marriage of opposites.

"Burdens are from God, and everything has a purpose," Abu Hasan smiled. "Especially suffering."

"But she is so very vile. . . ."

"Ah, you argued with her. You wanted to make her see the light, to change her! No, you should have kept your mouth shut. There is no winning with her."

"But God should have given you someone sweet and kind! God should not have given you so much suffering!"

"Ah, but if God hadn't mated me with her, hadn't taught me how to suffer her, how would I have gained the strength to tame this tiger?" laughed Abu Hasan. ✿

# III

# Pray

*Do not put musk on your body;*
*rub it on your heart.*
*What is musk?*
*The holy name*
*of the Glorious God.*

MATHNAWI, II, 267

◇⊢—◇—⊣◇

*By my hand*
*the seemingly impossible*
*is brought to pass,*
*and wings are restored*
*to the bird whose plumes*
*were torn away.*

MATHNAWI, II, 1917

# The Cup of Praise

*MATHNAWI, II, 1192-1214*

NE NIGHT, JALAMMUDIN, a rabab player and a singer, depressive and sorrowful by nature, was advised by his Mullah to pray regularly. Jalammudin could not see how so much muttering into one's beard could accomplish anything, let alone get rid of one's depression. But one night, mad and suicidal, he sat up and called out to God: "Allah! Allah! Allah!" he cried all night till his lips grew sweet with praise.

Iblis, the devil, said to him, "Stop this noisy babbling, like the braying of an ass! What does it accomplish? Do you hear anyone responding to you when you say, 'Allah! Allah! Allah!' Does your Allah ever say, 'Here I am'?"

"No," admitted Jalammudin.

"You're praying to someone who doesn't exist, you idiot. Why waste your breath?"

Broken hearted, Jalammudin ceased to call upon Allah. Now he was really alone, and there was no one he could turn to in his sorrow. Weeping in despair, he lay his head on a stone and fell asleep.

Jalammudin dreamed he was going somewhere, but kept stumbling on a large, cumbersome, thick iron chain that was entangled around his feet and legs. He came to a crystal clear pond and wanted to drink from it to assuage a fierce thirst, but couldn't. He saw why when he looked at his reflection in the pond and saw that the shackle of a lock, tied to the end of the chain, went through his lips and through his tongue.

In the distance, the invisible air coagulated into a form, and a man in flowing robes floated into the realm of matter from the Invisible. He came towards Jalammudin and stood before him. In his dream Jalammudin recognized him as Al Khadir, the guide to wayfarers and the creative spirit of rivers and greenery.

"Why didn't you pray before sleeping?" Al Khadir asked him.

Jalammudin wanted to say to Khadir, "But whenever I say 'Allah,' He never responds with 'Here I am.'" But all he could do was stammer and make growling sounds.

Knowing Jalammudin's heart, Al Khadir replied, "God has said, 'O human, every time you say *Allah*, I say *Here I am*. The two are not separate. Beneath every O *Lord* of yours is my *Here I am*.'"

Jalammudin motioned frantically to Al Khadir.

"Yes, I know you are thirsty. Listen, Jalammudin, I will tell you a story."

In his dream, Jalammudin sat up and listened to the tale.

"A depressed, sorrowful, doubt-filled man who was as thirsty as a fish sat on top of the high wall of a prison on the banks of a stream. He despaired of his life—of ever having his thirst quenched—for the wall was very high, and the stream was oh so very far away. Many times he thought about hurling himself from the heights and ending his life."

Jalammudin nodded furiously, as if to say the story resonated with him deeply.

"Suddenly the thirsty man wrenched a brick free from the masonry of the wall and hurled it at the stream," Al Khadir continued. "The sound of the water came to his ears like the voice of a long-forgotten beloved. It intoxicated him, like wine. The sound gave him so much relief and pleasure that he began to tear away the bricks of the wall of his prison with his bare hands and fling them at the stream. The sound of water to him was sweeter than the sound of the rabab, that most wonderful of musical instruments. It was like Israfil's trumpet on the day of resurrection, the sound of rain in a desert, the jangling of keys to a prisoner. With every brick he tore off, he came closer and closer to the water."

Muttering incoherently, Jalammudin got up and began to pull at his lock, but it stubbornly sealed his mouth as the chain entangled his legs.

"O Jalammudin! Prayer is the key! How then shall a thirsty, seeking man, fail to pray? Tear off with the hands of prayer the walls that keep you from the water, O despairing and desperate man!" Al Khadir said, looking deeply into Jalammudin's eyes and disappearing into them.

In the deep recesses of the shadows of his misty, dreaming mind, Jalammudin whispered silently to himself: "Allah!" Instantly, the lock on his mouth flung open, and the chains melted away to air. Jalammudin knelt on his knees and drank deep and long from the cool, clear pond. Having drunk his fill, he awoke from his dream.

The sun was about to rise in a sky filling with the first, soft colors of morning. A cool breeze was blowing in from the mountains. Jalammudin washed his hands and feet with water from a jar, brought out his prayer mat, sat reverently upon it, and quaffed fervently from the cup of praise. ॐ

# Moses Learns a Lesson

*MATHNAWI*, II, 1720-1791

HILE TRAVELING IN the wilderness early one morning, Moses heard the sound of a soulful flute coming from the rolling hills ahead of him. He followed its sound, and in a valley he came upon a youthful shepherd dancing nimbly and playing his flute amongst his herd of sheep in a beautiful grove of olive trees. The sharp outlines of the lichen-covered boulders, the dark and gnarled barks of the trees with their crisp leaves rustling softly in the breeze, the clear edges of the sheep with their curled horns, and the form of the bare-footed shepherd with his shining, curly hair down to his shoulders and a tunic that reached his knees, was such a brilliant and heartwarming picture that Moses sat and watched it for a while.

As Moses sat watching, the shepherd put his flute aside and dropped on his knees in a stance of impassioned prayer.

"O God, where are you? Tell me! I long for nothing more than to be your slave and serve you in every way. When you awake in the morning, I will bring you fresh milk, warm and foaming from my goats' udders. I will bathe you, wash your hair with water from the cool streams in the summer, and in the winter, collect firewood to heat your bathwater. I will comb your hair gently, get rid of the snarls, pick the lice as you sit in the sun and warm your bones, and after cooking you a meal with freshly ground corn flour, and freshly picked olives and greens, I will sew your shoes, darn your socks, mend your clothes, and sweep your room. And when you let me, I will rub your feet and kiss your hand. O ecstasy! O God, Friend, Beloved, you to whom I speak in my heart from morning till night, to whom I tell all my sorrows and my joys, and to whom I and all my goats are a sacrifice, tell me, O tell me, where are you?"

"Fool!" cried Moses, approaching him and hitting him with his staff. "Whom are you talking to?"

The shepherd was startled, and seeing the powerful presence of the Sage before him, he fell at Moses' feet.

"To the one who created me and my goats and these shrubs, and my eyes, and gave them light that I may see the world, and gave me hands to work, and a nose to smell the roses . . . To the one who is my companion in this wilderness and who my heart seeks through all its sorrows and bewilderment . . ."

"You speak like a fool and an unbeliever!" Moses yelled at him. "What babble is this? What blasphemy and raving? Your words smell of dung and decay. You have turned the silk robe of faith to rags! Does God have a mouth to drink your milk? Does God have a head with lice in it? Feet? Shoes? Is God your old and poor paternal uncle that needs looking after? Only he that lives and dies needs food and tending. Get up, idiot, and amend your thinking!"

The light went out of the shepherd's eyes at Moses' words. His shoulders slumped in grief and anguish and the landscape turned to endless vistas of sand with only the thin lines of dunes in the distance. He felt his entire world dissolving away.

Having chastised the ignorant shepherd, Moses carried on his way. He hadn't gone far when he heard God's voice thundering in his ears.

"Moses! Did you come as a prophet to unite or to break? You have parted my servant from me, and torn our hearts asunder."

"But . . . how could I have done that? I only spoke your truth. Humans limit you, Lord, by creating you in their own images."

"I have bestowed on everyone a way of believing and worshiping according to his understanding and temperament. What do I gain from worship? Nothing! Praying and worshiping is a kindness I have bestowed on my creatures so they may be tied to me with chords of love. The Hindu worships me in his own way, and the Jew in his. Let them pray any way they know how. I want only burning, burning, burning! He who is in love with that burning of separation is true to me! Do not seek rules or methods of worship, but love me however you can!"

When Moses heard these reproaches from God, he was stunned. God had just contradicted him, and God was always right. Confused, but always obedient to God's command, Moses ran down the hill to find the shepherd. But the olive grove was empty of goats and shepherd, the sound of song or flute. Moses found the footprints of the shepherd, and followed them hurriedly. Moses knew they were the shepherd's footprints because the footprints of a bewildered, distraught man are different from the footsteps of those who never burn. Sometimes they are one step ahead of the other, sometimes all zigzagged like the steps of a drunken man tottering in despair, and sometimes smudges, like the flopping belly of a fish on sand in search of water.

The shepherd had gone a long way away in his distracted state, and Moses had to climb a steep mountain to find him. Finally Moses saw him by a craggy, steep, harsh, jagged cliff, bare of vegetation. The shepherd was leaning on a staff, and his flock was nowhere in sight. Even the sheep and goats had given up at this height.

"Word has come!" Moses shouted to him as he climbed after him. "Word has come from God, O shepherd! Forgive me! Divine nature is intimate with human nature. Keep the fire of love raging in your soul. Say whatever your distressful heart desires, and give up rules and methods of worship. You are saved, and a whole world along with you. Come, come, return to your grove and your sheep, and worship God as you will!"

When the shepherd turned his face to him, Moses saw that he was no longer youthful. He had aged a lifetime, and the longing that had no name ravaged his face and eyes. There were vast distances and depths in his eyes that made the witness to them wheel about in infinite spaces with not a form or shape in sight.

"O Moses," the shepherd said in a deep and haunting voice. "I have passed beyond what I imagined. I have passed a hundred thousand years' journey on the other side. Your staff prodded me, and the horse of my body at first shied away, then bounded beyond the sky. I am full of gratitude to you. A thousand blessings upon your hand and rod for hitting me! I understand now that when I see an image in a mirror, it is my own image, and not the image in the mirror. Words and images no longer matter. Only silence. Only prayer."

He bowed to Moses, then turned and moved steadfastly towards the veiled summits of the mountains before him. ৯

# The Jug of Water

*MATHNAWI, I, 2252-2864*

N OLD BEDOUIN, Khalif, and his wife, Aziza, lived in the middle of the hot and arid desert. One night, while going to bed after the day's business, Aziza said to her husband, "The whole world is happy except us. We are the poorest of the poor. There is no bread in the house, we catch and eat gnats, our only sauce is anguish and envy, and our only drink, tears. We don't even possess rags! The burning sunshine of the desert clothes us, and moonshine is our blanket at night. I swear that if a wandering guest comes here tonight, I will steal even his tattered tunic as he sleeps."

"What is left of our life, beloved, that we should cause ourselves so much misery over what we don't have?" Khalif asked. "We are neither beautiful now, nor young. Our hair is grey, our skins wrinkled, and our bodies moving towards that great nothing from which we came. Are we going to spend the rest of this fleeting life pursuing wealth? Let us live patiently in wisdom's embrace. A rich or a poor life—neither endures. The wise do not attach themselves to the ups and downs of life, but stay above them."

"Ups? When have we known any ups? Wisdom is all very well, dear, for those whose bellies are full," Aziza said, with a sting in her voice. "But we are so poor that all our relatives and acquaintances have fled for fear I may ask them for a handful of lentils. The shopkeepers close their doors when they see me coming."

"You should ask God, instead of relatives and neighbors."

"God! Where is God? You call this a life? Especially now as we age we need some comfort and solace!"

"Stop complaining for a moment and listen, beloved," Khalif replied. "The dove on the tree utters thanks to God, even though she doesn't know if there's going to be any food tomorrow. The nightingale sings, trusting in her daily bread. We ought to stop complaining and pray for our desires to end."

"Desires!" scoffed Aziza. "I'll tell you what our desires would be—a roof to protect us from the elements, a goat to give us milk . . . milk!" she said, licking her dry lips. "Jars full of lentils, rice, couscous, healthy and fragrant herbs, and spices. A dress, good lord, joy to have a dress with no holes in it! A bangle of colored glass on my wrist, a small rug for the floor . . . oh even an iota more than just bare subsistence and animal need—a little bit of delight, of something that feeds my eye as well as my belly! I dare not even dream about desires!"

Aziza made a fist of her hand, and hit her belly with it in anger.

"These small sorrows are sent to us to test us, beloved. If we don't accept them, our lives will be poisoned. But if we accept them, then our whole life will be made sweet."

"Sweet!" cried Aziza.

"A husband and a wife are like a pair of shoes, Aziza. If one of the shoes is too tight, then both are useless to walk the Way. We have to give up our ego and anger. I want to march with a stout heart towards contentment and gratitude. Come, walk by my side."

"Contentment! You grab and eat locusts! You fight with dogs on the street for a bone! Haven't I seen you? All this talk of spiritual poverty is empty . . . posturing! Pomposity! Hypocrisy!"

"Oh woman, how little spiritual understanding you have! How little wisdom in your pea-sized brain! But what shall I expect from you? You are only a woman, beyond any reasoning, and made entirely of flesh and no spirit!"

"And where is your patience and wisdom when you spring upon your wife like a wild wolf, just because she's asking for a few little things to make life a little easier in her old age?"

"I regret the day I was mismatched with you!" Khalif shouted.

"And I with you, you disgrace to Arabs!"

"Materialist! All you can ever think of is money, money, money. Stuff, stuff, stuff!"

"Food, idiot! Food! Food!"

"I am sick of you! You are like a jug full of vinegar! In talking to you about spiritual things I am casting pearls before swine. Be silent, or I will leave this house and you in the morning!"

"House! You call this leaky, roofless thing a house? Fine, if you can't support me in these small matters, leave!"

Aziza and Khalif turned their backs to each other on their broken cot propped up with stones and mended with rags, but neither of them slept after their quarrel. Aziza tried through the night to imagine a life without Khalif, and was filled with desolation. For the first time after a long, long time, she prayed— not that her desires be eliminated, but fulfilled.

Khalif, too, was more disturbed than he would admit. He felt remorse at having spoken harshly to his wife, and was ashamed at the discovery that he was not as spiritually evolved as he had hoped. If he had been, would he not have stayed calm despite their differences?

In the morning, while Khalif was reluctantly packing a bag, and looking for a way out of his threat to leave home, Aziza threw herself at his feet, wept, and pleaded with him to stay.

"Without you, my beloved, the treasures of the world would mean nothing to me."

Khalif's heart melted like a wad of wax in fire when he heard these words. He lifted her up and embraced her.

"Forgive me. I'm so sorry and so ashamed at my harsh words.

You are the life of my soul, Aziza. When you are happy, I am happy. Tell me, what shall I do?"

"I prayed last night and have an idea. Go to the great, the merciful and generous Sultan of Baghdad. That great king will make you a king."

"I will do that if you say. But . . ." he asked after an agitated pause, "how can I go empty-handed to the king? What gift can I take him? We have nothing! And will he even consent to see a beggar like me?"

"Don't panic, my love. We have something that even the richest of kings don't have. This," she said, bringing down a jug with five spouts from a shelf.

"Oh," he cried in relief. "I had forgotten all about it!"

"When you live in the desert, there is nothing more precious than this!" Aziza said, with a sparkle in her eyes.

"Sew up the jug in felt that I may not spill it on the way, and the king may break his fast with our gift."

Aziza did so, and warning Khalif to keep the jug safe from highwaymen and boys throwing stones, she bid him goodbye as he began his journey to Baghdad.

After a long, hot, wearying journey through the desert in which, despite temptations, he kept the jug safe, Khalif arrived at the gate of the king in Baghdad. Surrounding the palace were magnificent rose gardens and meandering streams.

And all around the gate Khalif saw crowds of petitioners who had come to the king with hope in their hearts that their desires would be fulfilled. High and low, from Sheikhs to beggars, everyone waited their turn. While some were waiting to see him, others were carrying away loads of treasures and robes of honor.

And as Khalif stood there, clutching his jug sewn in a green rag, the sultan's officers motioned to him. Khalif turned around to see if they were calling someone else, but when he turned around, they were standing by him.

"Come! Come!" they said, warmly. "Bounty seeks beggars as much as beggars seek bounty!" And while Khalif stood there feeling shabby before them, they took him to the baths, bathed him in warm water with attar, rose water, jasmines, and then rubbed him down with almond oil. They clothed him in new garments that were soft and smooth against his skin. They made him a bed of silken sheets to rest upon, and before they left, Khalif gave them the jug to give to their king.

"Give this to the kind Sultan, so he may redeem his humble servant from poverty. It's sweet water. My wife collected this precious water from a ditch. And be careful with it. It's fragile, and I have carried it carefully a long, long way," Khalif said.

The officers smiled, but humbly accepted the jug as though it contained a rare elixir, for when you serve a great master, his qualities rub off on you.

Before falling asleep, Khalif rubbed his hands on the soft silk sheets, and thought of Aziza, and how pleased she would be with such luxury. Yes, he wanted to see her happy, and hoped the king would fulfill her desires.

Early in the morning, the officers took the jug to the sultan. He had just woken up when they presented the jug to him. When he heard the story, he took the jug in his hands and said to his smiling officers, "He brought me his most prized possession. How rare and beautiful this gift is!" Then he poured the dirty ditch water into a crystal chalice and quaffed it, to the amazement of his courtiers.

The sultan smacked his lips, as if it were the tastiest of wines, and said to his officers, "Go, fill this jug with gold and gems, and return it to the Bedouin. And give him robes of honor. And because he came to us the long way, through the desert, let him return the shorter way, by water. Make sure you see him home."

When Khalif awoke, his jug filled with gems and robes of honor were waiting for him in handsome traveling cases. He was in a daze, as if in a dream, as they mounted him on a horse and took him to the Tigris River.

Riding on the street on a well-caparisoned horse, Khalif was proud, both of himself and his wife, whose desires had sent him thither to such a generous king. Just being in the same town as the king had filled Khalif with a sense of well-being. He realized that his wife, with her material desires, and he, with his spiritual ones, were like the two wings that enable a bird to fly to Paradise. How happy she would be at his return with all this wealth!

Dismounting on the banks of the river, Khalif stood amazed and stunned. He had never, ever seen so much crystal clear water in his life, flowing by in endless, inexhaustible currents. Its expanse was so huge that large boats and barges with fishing nets bobbed upon it, and its bottom was strewn with pearls and precious stones.

Suddenly Khalif felt very ashamed. To have given such a king a jug of dirty water! Oh, what must he have thought! And oh, what utter generosity to return his piteous gift with pearls! He turned to the officers in a state of agitation, but their smiles reassured him.

"He broke his fast with the water from your jug," they said.

Khalif dropped to the ground and wept.

"Arise, Bedouin, and rejoice," they said. "Here everyone who comes with a desire is welcome. And each receives according to his request. Those that come for bread, receive bread and other viands. Those that seek material goods receive bags of pearls, and those that seek Truth, reach the Sea."

As Khalif stepped into a barge all decked out with a beautiful canopy in which sat four men with paddles, his heart sank suddenly and his eyes welled up with tears. Like an ass he had gone to the sultan to beg for straw! Why, oh why had he not asked to be given the gift of all gifts, that unseen rose garden beneath which Kawthar, the river of Paradise, flows, and on whose banks the saints, freed of all human desire, and anchored firmly in the eternal world, roam in leisure and in joy? Why had he not asked for the Truth and reached the Sea?

"Knock, knock on the door of Reality, Bedouin!" one of the rowers said to Khalif. "And know that it will be opened to you!"

The words rang in Khalif's ears and reassured him. Watching the play of light upon the waves of the water that carried him home to his beloved wife, he knew in his heart that the very proximity of the Sultan had set him on the Way: the river would eventually carry him to the Sea. ☙

# The Dark Flower of Justice

*MATHNAWI*, III, 2306-2503

VERYONE THOUGHT Nasirrudin, a young man without any kin, was very lazy. He made no pretense of his secret desire to make money without having to work for it.

"O God," he would pray, "give me riches without labor! It is you who have made me the way I am! I am sluggish and easily fatigued by the world's many requirements. I cannot bear the burdens of bosses and jobs. I like to move slowly through my day without any concern for time, just praying and reading, studying and sleeping, at liberty to do whatever I like whenever I like. Surely you who provide for people such as me can send me wealth that I might live in comfort and plenty, without any worries and hunger! Or at least, Lord, send me my daily bread. O King of Kings, you who provide sustenance to the embryo in the womb, fulfill my desire!"

People who were living by the sweat of their brows would speak derisively of Nasirrudin and think him very foolish, if not stupid. They were neither kind nor generous to him, so he was always hungry.

"God has provided you with a means of fulfilling your need, you scoundrel: use your hands and your feet and your mind!" they would say to him. Nevertheless, despite their ridicule and rudeness, Nasirrudin continued to trust in Providence's power to provide for him, and to pray for the fulfillment of his longing.

One morning, as he was praying fervently, somebody banged on his door with a great rattling, broke the bolt and the latch, and entered his room. It was a beautiful, fat cow with large horns, and Nasirrudin jumped up from his prayers, grabbed a rope, bound her feet with it, and without any qualms or mercy, slit her throat. Once she lay dead upon the floor, Nasirrudin went to fetch the butcher so he may help him rip off her beautiful hide. He would now have meat and money for a good while!

But the butcher knew the owner of the cow, Hamza, who soon arrived at Nasirrudin's door and yelled obscenities at him. "Return my cow, or pay me the price. Now!" he yelled.

"It's mine, and has been sent to me as an answer to my prayers," Nasirrudin replied. "The cow is not yours but a gift to me from God! Why else would she break open my door and enter my room this way?"

The owner of the cow was enraged beyond words. He caught Nasirrudin by his collar and proceeded to beat him black and blue. Then he threw him on his donkey and took him to King David, known far and wide for his impeccable justice.

"Please bestow some sense and intelligence into this criminal and imposter, Your Majesty," Hamza bowed to David. "My cow ran into his yard and his room, and he killed it! He can't revive her, and he won't pay me her worth! There is no doubt about where justice lies in this case! He's a lazy good for nothing, doesn't believe in labor, but lives off the sweat of others. Give me justice, my lord."

"And what do you have to say, young man?" David asked, looking into the eyes of the disheveled young man in a tattered cloak.

"I labor a great deal in my supplications, your Majesty," Nasirrudin replied. "The cow came to me in answer to my prayers."

"O good people! Gather around and hear his drivel!" Hamza cried.

"The owner of the cow is right!" they all yelled. "Replace the cow, pay up, or go to prison!"

Nasirrudin shut his eyes and prayed: "Oh you who have put these prayers on my tongue and in my heart, and raised my hopes, shield me, protect me from their wrath, even if I have erred."

"Well? Speak, noble one," David said to Nasirrudin.

The audience gasped. "Noble?! This lout, noble?"

"Why did you destroy the property of this honorable man?" David asked.

"Like Joseph, I am a dreamer, my lord." Nasirrudin replied. "Fate has thrust me into a deep dungeon and I escape it by my dreams. God is my friend in this dungeon and I pray to Him and I plead with Him night and day to send me a livelihood that is lawful."

"Lawful?!" Screamed the crowd. "What's lawful about killing another's cow?"

"I killed her so that I might give alms in thankfulness to Him who knows unseen things and answers prayers," Nasirrudin replied.

"Tell me," asked David, addressing himself to Nasirrudin, "did anyone give you this cow? Did you buy or inherit her? If not, you have performed an illegal act. If you haven't farmed, how do you expect to reap what you haven't sown? Go pay this good man his due. Borrow if you must, and labor away your dues."

"Long live our just and fair king, David!" the crowd shouted, as they surrounded Nasirrudin, ready to take him to prison if he did not make amends.

Nasirrudin lamented and wept in his heart. "Cast your light into David's heart, O Lord! Spare me the torture of life in prison, or what is worse, a life of drudgery," he prayed.

As David turned to leave, something about Nasirrudin's face rapt in prayer moved him deeply.

"Listen," David said, holding up his hand to the crowd. "Let the young man go. I need a day so I may go into a solitary place and seek advice from the Knower of Mysteries. Meditation opens a window through which the sunshine of grace pours upon me and shows me the Way."

Certain that the question of justice in this case was as clear as day, the crowd dispersed while David set off for the place where he would lock his doors and be entirely alone with Him who was closer to him than his jugular vein.

The next day, all the litigants returned to court and noisily awaited David's judgment.

They fell silent as David entered the hall.

The king looked at the plaintiff and said, "Demand justice only if you deserve justice. Give up your claim to the cow, Hamza. Go home, and live in peace. If you refuse to do this, a worse fate will befall you."

Hamza and the crowd were in an uproar. King David has lost his mind, they muttered, before loudly demanding justice and an explanation for this absurd judgment.

"I'm warning you, Hamza. Shut your eyes and look within yourself for the answer. If you find yourself utterly blameless, then we shall speak of justice."

"What have I ever done to deserve this?" Hamza shouted. "It's all as clear as the nose on my face!"

Hamza's speech incited the crowd to anger.

"Silent!" David said. "You have not taken my advice to go home and live in peace. So now I say, Hamza, give this young man, Nasirrudin, all your wealth: all your cows, and all your camels. If not, you shall fare even worse than this."

"Insult to injury!" cried Hamza, pulling out his hair. "Listen, O people, the wise king has become a fool!"

"Your children and your wife are also now Nasirrudin's slaves. Even now, O unconscious man, incapable of introspecting and remembering your crimes, go home and live in peace!"

But David's words only put Hamza in a crazy frenzy, tearing at his garments, running from end to end of the hall, glaring with rolling eyes at the king, and screaming.

"Hark ye, hark ye, the time of injustice has come!"

"O king!" the people shouted, "This is unworthy of you! How can you treat an innocent man thus? What faith will we have in you after this manifestly unjust judgment?"

"Come, all, let us get to the root of this issue. Come, bring shovels, and follow me! But tie up this criminal, Hamza, so he doesn't escape from justice," King David said.

Bewildered and curious, the crowd, with Hamza bound hand and foot, followed David to the outskirts of the town where in a plain field stood a huge tree with wide spreading branches. David paused beneath it, and pointed to dark red flowers by the trunk of the tree.

"You demand the law. Here it is. You want to confess, Hamza?"

"To what? To what must I confess?" Hamza spat.

"O unreflecting man! You, you killed Nasirrudin's grandfather and his only son, Nasirrudin's father, and buried them here."

Hamza strained against his chains while the crowd shouted, "What evidence do we have of this dastardly allegation?"

"What proof, indeed?" Hamza shouted.

"Ask him," David said.

"I did nothing of the sort!" Hamza said indignantly.

"Blood sleeps not, nor forgets. The sown seed shoots up from the loam. Hamza was Nasirrudin's grandfather's slave. After killing his grandfather and father, this scoundrel abandoned the little orphan grandson, this young man here, and appropriated everything of his master's: wives, slaves, animals, property, wealth."

"But how do we know for sure?" the crowd asked.

"Dig up the earth here and find their skeletons. Nothing can be hidden from God's eye. Here, dig here where these red flowers have grown from the blood."

And sure enough, two skeletons were discovered deep in the earth, together with a knife bearing Hamza's name.

"Evil will out," King David said. "No one can hide from the sight of God. There is a justice greater than ours. This man made a noise about one cow, when he himself took his master's hundred cows and hundred camels. Never once did he supplicate with God, or open his heart to Him. Come, O demander of justice, receive it. "

There was no restraining the crowd's fury. Like a wild animal with many hands and feet, it fell upon Hamza and dispatched him with his own knife. The wicked man was killed and King David's subjects henceforth began to look within themselves for answers, and to supplicate and pray when they were bewildered and lost.

"Come," David said, putting his arm around the young Nasirrudin's shoulders, walking back into town. "Enjoy now the fulfillment of the desire placed in you by the mysterious Lord of Justice." ♠

# IV

## Be Content

*One feeling*
*of contentment*
*is better than a hundred*
*viands and trays of food.*

*MATHNAWI, VI, 3784*

◊╫──◊──╫◊

*Believers are the laziest folk*
*in the two worlds,*
*because they get their harvest*
*without plowing,*
*since God is working for them.*

*MATHNAWI, VI, 4886*

# The All-Knowing Rooster

*MATHNAWI*, III, 3266-3389

HWAJA MIRZA, a young man eager to advance further and further in the material as well as spiritual spheres, said to Moses:"You have so much spiritual power; teach me something of great value. I would like to live as the wise animals live, without anxiety or fear of death. I have a rooster who I am going to have for dinner one of these days, but he goes around crowing and strutting, fanning his feathers and preening, with not a care in the world. I have a dog, too, a bit skinny, and not a very good watchdog because all he thinks about is food, but he sleeps peacefully on his rug and plays with abandon. I constantly worry about today and tomorrow. I have tried many spiritual techniques to rid me of this habit, but none of them have worked. Moses, Lord, Miracle Maker, teach me how to understand the animals' language, so I may become a peaceful, playful man who does not think about tomorrow."

"It's not so easy, Khwaja Mirza," Moses replied. "This desire of yours to learn the language of the beasts is full of dangers. God has given humans this limitation for a reason. You can learn everything from saints and from God himself, who always speaks to us through our hearts. Give up this vain desire, Mirza, return home, and live in peace and praise for the rest of your days, content with what you have."

"For the rest of my days?" thought Mirza, spiraling down in a maelstrom of worry. "What does Moses mean? That I don't have long to live? And what does he mean by asking me to be 'content?' That I will not make any more money? Knowing the language of animals will make me millions. I'm the richest man in town, but it isn't enough."

Aloud he said, "I beseech you, Moses, let me hear and understand the speech of animals.

I have a great desire for this, and surely God has a reason to give me this desire. Even if I have just a few days more to live, I would die peacefully. I have reconciled myself to death, but try as I might, I cannot accept that this particular desire of mine may never be fulfilled. O generous one, do not disappoint me in this!"

For a long time Moses, cognizant of the dangers inherent in the extraordinary ability to comprehend the speech of animals, dissuaded Mirza from his craving. But weary of Mirza's unremitting importunities, Moses granted the young man his desire with an admonition: "Change your mind even now, Mirza, for such power does not suit everyone. A recognition of one's limitations and humility in the face of the mystery of life is the appropriate attitude of the devout."

"Please, I beg of you. I will take the consequences of my desire. It is my life's goal to have this ability. I have been praying fervently for it!"

"The power of prayer is strong, Mirza. Be very careful what you pray for. You might regret it!"

"You always say we have free choice. At least let me understand the speech of my dog and my rooster, my horse and mule."

"So be it. When the blackness of night turns to a dark indigo in which stars are still bright, when a cool breeze blows in from the mountains, and when your rooster crows, you will have the power. But don't complain to me later if you are not happy with your coveted prize."

Generally a late sleeper, Mirza awoke early the next day, eager to test his powers. Instead of the usual *cook-a-roon-ka-doooon*, *cook-a-roon-ka-doonoon*, he heard his cock say: "Awake! Awake! O sleepers! Do your ablutions, and pray, pray, pray! Time is passing away, O sleepers, awake and begin your day!"

Mirza rushed downstairs from his bedroom in excitement. He wanted to be there when his dog spoke. But he was just lying about on the mat, his forelegs and back legs splayed, his belly and muzzle flush against the floor, his beady eyes open and eagerly awaiting his meal. The maid, who was cleaning the dining room just then, did not like dogs, so was very lax in feeding him. Often she ate the food the cook prepared for the dog and did not feed him at all. Now, as she shook out the tablecloth, a crumb from last night's dinner fell to the floor. But by the time the dog mustered together his limbs to reach the crumb, the rooster had already snatched it up and swallowed it.

"You," Mirza heard the dog say to the rooster, "are unjust and unfair! That crumb belonged to me! You can eat grain and corn, and the maid feeds you generously, but I have been waiting all night for that crumb! You are greedy and fat! Look at me! I am all bones!"

"Listen to me and be patient," the rooster replied. "Our Khwaja's horse is going to die tomorrow, and you will have a feast! You can fatten yourself to your heart's content on his organs."

Mirza's excitement turned to agitation. His beautiful, fast, and strong, expensive horse was the envy of his townspeople! What a loss! What was he to do? As Mirza stood there, his turmoil shaped itself into a clever scheme: he would sell the horse today! Let someone else take the loss! He had been right! He could benefit materially from his extraordinary spiritual powers.

He rushed to his stable where the animals stood in their stalls, and hurriedly began to saddle and bit the horse.

"What's with him?" the horse said to the mule. "He's never up this early. And today of all days, when I don't feel like doing much. I have an ache in my bones."

"Strange you should say that. I'm not feeling too perky myself this morning," the mule replied. "I'm glad he hasn't come to load me down, the greedy miser. Makes us do more than we can and doesn't even treat us well. Straw is all I get, never a few oats now and then. At least he grooms you, and . . ."

"Only because he likes to hear people admire me, not for any love, the shallow imbecile!"

Mirza's anger at his animals was tempered by his knowledge of the horse's impending death. He rode him hard to the market, whipping and prodding him with his heel, and to his delight, sold him off for twice as much as he had paid for him.

"You have cheated me of my crumb!" barked the dog to the rooster the next day as Mirza stood by and listened. "Where is the feast you promised me? The horse is gone!"

"He died elsewhere. I am sorry about that. Our owner was lucky this time. Someone else suffered the loss instead of him. But I promise that his mule will die tomorrow. That, too, will be good news for dogs. Go lie down now, and don't complain too much."

Mirza went straightaway to the stable, took the mule to the market, and sold him off, gloating at his ability to forestall loss and misfortune.

"Liar!" cried the dog the next day. "Where is your promise, and where is my feast?"

Before the rooster could reply, the buyers of the horse and the mule came to the house and reported to Mirza that the horse and mule had died suddenly, and that their dogs had feasted upon them.

"See? I'm not a liar. I'm sorry, but listen carefully," Mirza heard the rooster say. "Our Khwaja's slave is going to die tomorrow."

"And what good will that do me?" The dog growled.

"The slave's relatives will distribute bread to the dogs and the beggars," the rooster replied.

"Bread is not meat, and how in hell do you know all of this, anyway?"

"I'm a cock. I know that any minute my head can be lopped off and my body thrown into a pot of boiling water, together with onions, garlic, and other spices. I am reconciled to being someone's dinner because I know I cannot go before my time, and nothing can prevent my slaughter when my time has come. We roosters have a great trust in the timing of the universe. I had a brother whose head was cut off and he still didn't die! He lived for two more years because his time had not come. His master fed him through a tube and made a lot of money showing him off in fairs and circuses. And only when his time had come did he keel over and become soup. It is only by embracing death fully and whole heartedly that we can live a carefree, joyous life full of foresight."

Mirza was too distracted in his hurry to sell off his slave to pay heed to the rooster's wisdom. He returned home and heaved a big sigh of relief before going to bed that night. He had paid a lot of money for his slave, and was thrilled at having sold him for even more than he had bought him for. Through his precious talent to comprehend his animals, he had avoided so many calamities, and even gained from them! Mirza slept very well that night.

He awoke the next morning to another squabble between the dog and the rooster. Hungry, getting leaner and feebler, the dog barked in rage and chased the rooster all around the courtyard, threatening to eat him raw, feathers and all. The rooster flew up on a wall, and perched safely at a height, shouted down to the dog.

"I promise! The foolish and deluded Khwaja has passed on his losses to others, not knowing that every loss inflicted on us by destiny prevents and circumvents other losses; that all of our misfortunes are sent to us from God, who knows best. If the Khwaja had let his horse die, as was the will of God, he would have saved his mule and his slave. But he increased his wealth at the cost of his own life. Today, soon, the Khwaja will die, and in mourning for him, his heir will slaughter a cow. Feast to your heart's fill, dog. This is a certainty!"

Distracted and anguished beyond words, Mirza ran to Moses and knocked furiously on his door.

"Save me, save me, I beg you, save me, O merciful one!" he said, falling at Moses' feet and sobbing with fear. "I repent!

I repent! Take back the gift; make me ignorant of the future. Let me submit to God's will humbly, but please, please, save me!"

"Go sell yourself and escape," Moses said. "You are an expert now in avoiding losses, so jump out of the well of death. Pass on your death to others, too, O Khwaja."

"Do not rub this in my face, O please; do not beat me over the head with my terrible mistake. Just save me!"

"An arrow shot from the bow does not return at one's bidding. All I can do is pray that you die in peace, with faith and trust in your heart in the workings of the universe."

Mirza doubled over in pain. Death's wings had brushed against him, and there was no saving him now. As Moses' disciples carried the Khwaja home on a stretcher so he could die in his own bed, Moses prayed.

"O God, in your mercy, forgive him his transgressions! And from his example let others learn to be content and to know that you alone know the right course." ⚘

# Bones

MATHNAWI, II, 145-155; 456-465

AN, AN AGING MAN, was hounded by one overwhelming desire: to learn the magic that brought the dead back to life. He believed that God had made a terrible mistake by inventing death. Even more than the loss of dear ones, Jan could not reconcile to losing his senses, which he loved and lived for. His favorite sense was taste; food gave him great pleasure and joy, and he couldn't imagine a time when he would have to forego eating. The thought of it sent him into paroxysms of anguish.

Jan had heard about Jesus' recent resurrection of Lazarus. How he wished he had been present when Lazarus rose from his tomb! To be in the presence of the mystery of mysteries! To have heard the magic formula and be able to practice it! To be able to transform bones back to living and breathing flesh . . . to sight, and sound, smell and touch, and taste! To be able to do what God could do, but better! In Jan's version of the world, there would be no death. No—all would be immortal.

Jan resolved to find Jesus and follow him until his wish to learn the magic incantation was granted. Wherever Jesus went, Jan followed him like a dark shadow, pleading and begging: "O exalted one, teach me the words that would bring the dead back to life. I would like to learn to do this so I can do good service and relieve mankind of its greatest grief: separation from loved ones."

Jesus knew that Jan desired the tremendous power such magic would bestow upon him. "Be content with what you know and do not know, have or do not have, Jan. It is not your work to go against the commands of God."

But Jan doggedly persisted in his request, pleading and cajoling Jesus day in and day out. One day as Jesus was resting from his travels under the shade of a tree, Jan, who had been hounding him as usual, saw some bones in a nearby pit. His craving flared up and once again he begged Jesus to teach him the magic whereby he may be able to clothe the skeleton with flesh and bring it back to life.

"Your breath would need to be purer than the purest rain, and your consciousness as clear as angels' hearts for you to learn it," Jesus said.

"How may I learn to make myself so pure and clear?" Jan asked.

"Many lifetimes of submission," Jesus answered. "And when you get to the point of such purity your desire would be only and forever to obey the highest laws."

"Please! If you don't want to teach it to me, at least restore these bones to life," Jan said, hoping to memorize the words as Jesus uttered them, learn them, and thus be able to circumvent his own death.

Jesus, tired of Jan's repeated pleadings, shut his eyes and was silent for a long time.

"What are you doing, Lord?" Jan asked, impatient and curious.

"Consulting God," Jesus replied.

"And did He agree to my request?"

"He said to give you what you want, for your time has come," replied Jesus.

"To . . . die?"

"Yes."

"No, no, you mistook God's meaning, Lord Jesus. He must have meant it is time for me to learn the magic," Jan insisted. He wanted to ask Jesus the contents of his entire conversation with God, but his impatience to see the bones come to life made him desist.

"Unless a corn of wheat falls on the ground and dies, it lives alone. But if it dies, it brings forth much fruit," Jesus said.

Jan fell at Jesus' feet. "I don't understand your meaning, but please fulfill my dream and bring these bones to life. I beg you!"

"You have the choice to turn away from your desire or succumb to your fate," Jesus said, kindly.

"It's all I ever wanted! Please!"

Jesus looked at Jan with compassion, and then stood by the bones. Alert, ready to grasp the words that Jesus was about to pronounce upon the bones, Jan stood excitedly by the edge of the pit.

But no words issued from Jesus' mouth. His breath was sufficient for the purpose. The bones that lay randomly on the earth, covered with dust, began to stir before his eyes and came together in a pattern: the vertebrae in a straight line, the hip, thigh, and leg bones beneath them, the skull, eye sockets, and shoulder blades above them. But it was all happening too slowly for Jan. With one eye on the goings on in the pit, he asked Jesus the question he had been itching to ask about his consultation with God.

"What else did God say?"

"I asked him what I should do with you, and God said, 'The thistle that has grown in him is the consequence of his own sowing.'"

"What does that mean?" Jan asked, watching with fascination the coming together of molecules to make the meat that covered the skeleton. Jesus said something in reply, but Jan's attention was grabbed by the spectacle before him: the flesh was coming together in a form that he couldn't recognize . . . something was not quite right . . . something dark and black was growing on it . . . hair . . . black hair, not the hair of a man, but soft fur, as on a dog or on a horse. Were these the bones of an animal? Jan began to feel the dark clouds of disappointment gather in his heart. It was a dog . . . a large dog. Or was it a bear?

Jan took a few hurried steps backward . . . but before he could go very far, whatever it was sprang at him . . . Jan only had a quick glimpse . . . mane . . . teeth . . . a deep, dark maw . . . the red, blazing eyes of a black lion . . . .

"Alas, those that persist in their perverse desires are seeking their own destruction." Jesus' words came clearly into Jan's ears, before the lion sprang upon him, struck him with his paw, tore open his skull, scattered his brain on the spot, and then lay meekly at Jesus' feet.

Jesus looked at the spectacle before him with sadness in his heart. He shut his eyes and prayed for Jan's soul. Then he turned to the lion and asked, "Why did you kill him so quickly?"

"Because he was a fool to mistrust the hereafter. And his greatest folly consisted in this: he met you, Lord of the Living Waters, and asked for nothing more than magic, when he could have reached the Sea!"

"And why, after killing him, do you not eat him?"

"Because," replied the lion, "I have already eaten my allotted portion of food in the world. I was a slave to my hungers when I was alive, but prefer to live in Paradise, where no hungers remain. I am supremely content with my state. O Lord, now that I have performed your task, turn me back into bones, and return me to my home in the Unseen!" ҉

# Og, the Hungry Giant

MATHNAWI, V, 64-286

RAVELERS CAME TO a mosque in the evening and asked Mustafa, the Prophet Mohammed (may the blessings of Allah be upon him), for hospitality. Mohammed told his companions, "Let us divide these guests amongst us, take them home, feed and house them."

Each of Mustafa's companions chose a guest and took him home. But no one was willing to take Og, an ugly, fat, giant of a man with a dirty, heavy bag on his shoulder. When he walked, the fat around his belly flopped like a sack, and his backside shook and shivered. He smelled, too, because there was dirt in the many folds of his skin that his short and stubby arms couldn't reach. Because he was left behind like dregs, Mustafa took him home.

The women of his household were upset with Mustafa for bringing Og home. When they began their evening meal, Og put down his bag, lifted up the bucket that contained the milk of seven goats, and guzzled it all down. But it wasn't enough to fill him up. When the rice, lentils, and bread were brought out, Og grabbed everything and shoveled it into his mouth, making smacking and gurgling noises and snorting like a pig. He took some leftover bread and put it in his bag. After he had devoured everything, he sat upon his haunches and released loud and noisy sounds from his body.

The women of the household were disgusted, angry, and in an uproar. Everybody, including the servants, would go hungry that night.

After dinner, Mustafa showed Og to his room. While Og picked his teeth like a bear after a huge meal, Mustafa put clean sheets on the bed for his guest. He bid Og a pleasant sleep, and left so his guest could get some rest.

One of the maids was so angry with Og for depriving her of her meal that she bolted the door of his room from the outside and locked it.

At night Og felt rumblings and cramps in his belly from having eaten too much. He hastened to the door, but found it shut. He tried several times to open the door with his might, to take it right off its hinges, but the door was sturdy and would not budge. Doubled over in discomfort and pain, Og lay back on his bed and dreamt he was alone in a desert. He went behind a boulder and relieved himself. A powerful stench awoke him from his dream, and he discovered that he had soiled his bed. He lay in the mess all night, trapped in his own filth and terrible smell. Og, ashamed of himself, hoped to flee before his hosts discovered him in this pitiful state. He longed for dawn, longed to be clean. All night he strained to hear the sound of the bolt lifting.

In the early hours of the morning, when a few stars still twinkled in the sapphire sky, Mustafa awoke to a dreadful smell. He knew it was coming from Og's room, so he went to his door, unlocked it, lifted the bolt, and stood behind the door so that Og could escape without being seen. Mustafa wanted to save his guest from shame and disgrace.

Hearing the bolt lift, Og arose from his bed and fled out of the room, through the courtyard, and out into the street.

As Mustafa entered the room, the maid followed him, her nose covered with the palm of her hand, and her face screwed up in a grimace.

"Look what he has done, the beast!" she cried. "Who is going to clean this up? Not me!"

"Bring me a bucket full of water, some soap, and the washing bat, and I will clean them," Mustafa said.

"Oh but . . ." the maid pretended to protest, but Mustafa insisted, so she fetched him the objects he had requested.

Meanwhile, it wasn't too long before Og's hunger made him realize that in his hurry to flee, he had left his food bag behind in the room. He hoped everyone would still be asleep and he could retrieve it without being discovered.

He stepped into the courtyard, and there sat Mustafa on his haunches by the drain, his face glowing in the first light of day, cheerfully washing the sheets from Og's bed.

The sight astounded Og. He stood still, and as he watched Mustafa's calm, humble, kind face as he washed the filth out of the sheets, a great agitation and self-loathing arose in his heart. He beat his belly and his face with his hands, and then banged his head against the wall.

"Oh head without understanding. Oh tongue and belly without restraint. Oh breast without light!" he bellowed in pain and self-disgust.

Mustafa washed his hands and stood up. He opened his arms and said to Og, "Come here."

Og came towards him as if he was awoken from heavy sleep. Mustafa took him in his arms and quieted the giant. Og was overcome, and Mustafa's touch opened Og's inner eye so he could see how misled he had been in all his beliefs.

Og had always thought that there was no other truth than food and drink and the pleasure derived from them. Only the things you could touch, taste, and hold were real and everything else an illusion. His lack of faith in all things spiritual had created an insatiable hunger for food. The more he ate, the hungrier he became, and the more his belly asked for "More! More! More!" Just like the devil had seduced Adam with an ear of wheat, he had seduced Og with greed. Every moment, the

Evil One took hold of Og's ears and understanding as though they were the ears of a horse, and pulled him away from the Way, towards gluttony.

"Come to yourself for there are great things to be done here, Og. You can't make a pilgrimage to paradise if you are loaded down. The body is your riding beast and needs to be treated with love and kindness."

"I am weary of this unreal existence," Og sobbed. "I want to fill the emptiness of my doubt with prayer and continence. I have filled myself with dung!"

"When the body empties itself of dung, Allah fills it with musk and glorious pearls," Mustafa said, and sprinkled water on Og's head. He bathed Og and gave him clean white robes to wear. A great rapture arose in Og's heart after he was cleansed in Mustafa's river of healing.

Mustafa said, "Be my guest tonight also, Og."

"By Allah," Og replied, "I am your guest forevermore. I will eat at your table in this world and the next, Mustafa."

That night, Og drank half the milk from a single goat, and then closed his lips. All the people of Mustafa's household were astonished that this huge lamp was filled by one drop of oil.

The prophet offered him more milk and bread, but Og turned them down.

"Last night I starved," Og said, "but tonight I am full." ❧

# The Sweetness of Bitter Melons

MATHNAWI, II, 1462-1532

HOUGH LUQMAN was a slave, he was a master of himself because he was free of anger, lust, resentments, greed, and pride. His enlightened king, Hamid, who could discern the difference between chaff and grain, appearance and truth, had seen through Luqman's role as slave to his inner state and loved him dearly. King Hamid was quite weary of the constricting role of master, and found great joy in humble service to his slave and beloved, Luqman.

King Hamid would have set Luqman free a long time ago, but Luqman, who liked being slave to a king such as Hamid, did not want to be free. Whenever the king went to a place where he was not known, he would place Luqman on his own horse, and travel behind him on an ass, like a slave. King Hamid would put his own clothes on Luqman, wear the latter's clothes, and serve him. When the king's cooks prepared feasts for him, or when his friends and subjects brought him delicacies from all over the world, he would feed Luqman with his own hands before partaking of it himself. His greatest delight was eating Luqman's leftovers. If Luqman did not eat, the master would also forego his food. Such was his love for his slave.

One day, King Hamid received a basket of the best melons from the Punjab in India. They were reputed to be the sweetest in the world, and when cut, showed the brightest saffron. Before tasting any himself, King Hamid sent for Luqman, and when he arrived, seated him on a cushion on his own chair. When the master cut a slice and gave it to Luqman on his own gold plate, Luqman ate it with such relish, such slurping of its juices, that everyone present craved a slice, too. The master gave him another slice, and Luqman ate it the same way. The master continued to offer him slices, and Luqman continued to eat them with great pleasure. When Luqman was surfeited, King Hamid decided to eat some himself.

As soon as the king bit into it, however, his face puckered up with distaste and he spat the melon out. His tongue was blistered and his throat was burned with its bitterness. He threw his hands up in pain and distraction, and cried out to his slave:

"Oh, how did you eat this again and again? Why didn't you complain? How did you turn so much poison to sweetness?"

"From your generous hand and bounty, O master," Luqman replied, "I have received so many gifts. Tell me, how can I complain about one bitter thing? Bitter or sweet, I am content to eat whatever you delight in giving me, my master."

"But how could you endure the bitterness of slice after slice?" The master asked.

"By love, my master, bitter things become sweet. By love, iron becomes gold, pain becomes healing, the hungry man content, the dead man made living," Luqman replied.

"And a burdened king a joyous slave," said King Hamid, bowing before Luqman and kissing his feet. ✿

# v

# Trust Spiritual
Masters

We drink the water of Khizr
from the river of
the speech of saints:
Come, O heedless, thirsty man!

*MATHNAWI*, III, 4302

◇⊩—※—⊩◇

Become like Solomon,
in order that thy demons
may hew stone
for thy palace.

*MATHNAWI*, IV, 1149

# ꞁop Up on ꞁꝶy ꞁump

*MATHNAWI*, II, 3436-3455

 LITTLE MOUSE, FULL of self-confidence, considered himself a great hero because he often did things no other mouse would dare to do. He knew that even though he was tiny, he was really a lion at heart. He always extricated himself from the direst of circumstances using his wits, and came out stronger and braver. All the other mice were full of admiration for him.

One night, while scurrying across the sands on his way home from foreign lands, the mouse almost strangled himself by getting entangled in the leading-rope of a sleeping camel. At first the mouse felt a little flustered at his predicament, but he soon managed to free himself after some effort. Upon seeing the end of the rope, the mouse had a brilliant idea.

"Ah-ha!" he thought, congratulating himself. "Wait till they see this!"

The mouse took the end of the rope and tugged at it. The rope straightened out, the sleepy camel got up and began to follow the mouse as he led him through the night over hill and plain.

"I am going to arrive home leading a camel!" the mouse chuckled to himself over and over. "How they will watch, wonder, and applaud!"

All went well till the mouse came to a raging river at which even the stoutest and bravest of lions and wolves would have lost heart.

Day was dawning as the mouse stood on the banks, deliberating what to do.

"O my leader," said the camel, opening an eye. "Why stand still now, O brave and clever young mouse? Step into the river like a hero, O my guide, and carry us across."

"This is a wide and deep river, O ship of the desert. I am afraid to drown," the mouse replied.

"Not as deep as you think, O leader," the camel said, stepping into the river. "See? It is only up to my knees. Why do you fear?"

"There are differences between one knee and another," the mouse said, marveling at how such a large animal as a camel could be so stupid as not to know the relativity of size. "It is only up to *your* knee, but it is a thousand ells higher than the tip of my head."

"But you are cleverer than I. Your cleverness and bravery will save you, O leader. Venture out into the waters, and I will follow. You will save us yet."

Not wanting to lose face before a stupid camel, the mouse took the rope in his mouth, and ventured out one step into the river. "I can always scramble back on the rope to the shore," he thought to himself.

But the raging currents of the swift river carried him downstream struggling and grasping. The line, however, saved him. Shivering, thoroughly wet, and half dead, he clamored ashore and collapsed near the camel's foot.

"Next time do not rely on your lion-heartedness, but trust in those who can see further than you, O mouse. Cleverness will drown you. Do not think you can lead the guide who no obstacle can deter from the Way," the camel said, looking down with compassion and pity at the wet rag of a mouse gasping for breath. "This passage is easy and safe for me. I can ferry a thousand of you across. Come, hop up on my hump, and I'll take you home." ꕀ

# I Am a Mirror

*MATHNAWI, I, 2365-2370*

HE PROPHET MOHAMMED, may peace be upon him, sat silently beneath the date palms one evening. Some of his disciples and other men from the nearby village sat by him. They had just finished a meal of the season's first *rohtab*, soft, sweet white dates, and fresh goats' milk. Cool breezes blew in from the oasis as the sky turned a bright tourmaline with hues of pink and blue in which the thin ribbon of the new moon shone with Venus in its hollow.

"Mohammed," Jahl called, breaking the silence and standing up with a quick and agitated movement. Putting his hand on his sword, Jahl broke into jarring speech that made everyone suddenly alert. "Your great grandfather, Hashim, was an ugly and evil man, and his sons have also spawned ugly sons!"

Haider, Mohammed's most passionate disciple, drew his sword and was about to spring on Jahl for insulting his prophet, when Mohammed said, calmly, "You are right, Jahl. You have spoken the truth."

Speechless and disappointed, but silenced by Mohammed's words, Haider sheathed his sword. Jahl had been getting ruder and more insolent over time. Nothing would have given him more satisfaction than putting his sword through Jahl and watching the sand soak up his rude and impertinent blood.

Some time elapsed in silence, then Abu Bakr said, bowing before Mohammad, "O Sun, descendant of the destroyer of evil, Hashim, your grandfather, storehouse of virtue and bravery, was a courageous and beautiful man, as you are!"

Mohammed turned to him, and said, "You have spoken the truth, Abu Bakr."

Another silence followed. Haider could refrain himself no more, and he burst out: "How can it be that both of them with their opposite views are speaking the truth?"

"You have also spoken the truth," Mohammed said, smiling at the young man. "I am a mirror, Haider, polished by the divine hand. People see their own images in me. The world appears blue through a blue glass, red through a red. Everything they see is a reflection of themselves."

· "Is there no truth in the world, then?" Haider cried. "Is nothing real?"

"Purify yourself of your passions, Haider, if you seek the Real. Polish your heart till it becomes a white and colorless mirror. Then truth will shine through you," the prophet said, putting his arms around Haider's shoulders. 繠

# The House of God

MATHNAWI, II, 2216-2251

HEN BAYAZID WAS just a young Sheikh, and not the revered saint he would later become, he was in a hurry to get to Mecca for the great pilgrimage, Hajj. He organized a small but well-provisioned caravan, and set off through the desert with hope in his heart. By circumambulating the shrine in the center of the Kaaba, the great mosque, seven times and kissing the sacred black stone, he knew he would find God and everlasting life.

Bayazid would search for holy men in each town he stopped in on the way to Mecca. He knew that the *abdal* (saints) were the true treasures of the world; that their breath and words, like spring rain, grew gardens with fragrant roses in human hearts open to their guidance. He wanted to become like dust under the feet of the men of God.

Bayazid's intuition led him unerringly to holy men wherever he went. When he stopped in a town for the night, his search brought him to a dilapidated hut on the edge of town. It was evening, and the heat of the day had abated a bit. Abu Aziz sat on a sagging cot under a palm tree in his courtyard, surrounded by small children of all ages in dirty rags, clamoring on his knees and sitting in his lap. A skinny goat was tethered in one corner, and in another an aging woman was sitting before the kitchen fire, stoking it with kindling and blowing on the coals through a pipe.

Abu Aziz was a blind old man bent with age, like the crescent moon. Bayazid perceived that in his blindness he saw more than the sighted could see with a million eyes. Abu Aziz's entire being, radiant with light, was like a window through which light dawned in Bayazid's soul.

Bayazid alighted from his camel, bowed deeply to Abu Aziz, and sat on the ground before him. After names and pleasantries were exchanged, Abu Aziz asked, "Where are you going, O man of God, Bayazid?"

"At daybreak I leave for Mecca, Holy One."

"Why?"

"Allah in the Koran has commanded all Muslims to make the Great Pilgrimage."

"Mecca is a long way from here, Bayazid. And what provisions have you taken for the road?"

"Two hundred silver dirhams that are sewed into the lining of my robe."

"And what will you do in Mecca?"

"I will circumambulate the Kaaba seven times and kiss the sacred black stone."

"Then circle me seven times, kiss me, lay those dirhams before me, O generous one, and consider your goal accomplished, Bayazid. Know that this is the greater pilgrimage and that your desire has been fulfilled."

Bayazid was a little taken aback. Many thoughts and doubts jostled in his head about the old man's request. Abu Aziz was a poor, aging, disheveled, ragged old man, looking up at him with the blind whites of his eyes rolling in his head. This? God? Impossible, impossible, Bayazid's eyes were screaming. Was this a temptation that he, Bayazid, on his way to meet God, had to overcome?

"I swear that God has chosen me above his House," Abu Aziz continued. "Although the Kaaba is the house of religious service, my form too, is the house of His inmost consciousness. The Living God lives in this house, which is my body. I am the Kaaba, Bayazid. When you have seen me, you have seen God. To serve me is to obey and glorify God. Open your eyes well and look at me so you may behold the Light of God in man. Beware, do not think God is separate from humans."

As Bayazid stood in the presence of the old man, a marvelous change began to happen to him. Doors opened in his head and heart that let in fragrant breezes from the land of the Unseen, breezes that lifted the veil of unreality, loosed the knots of his doubts and fears, and infused him with a knowledge far more certain than the evidence of his eyes. Bayazid understood that all his doubts were chains his mind had conjured up to keep him shackled to duality. He saw the Unity in which God and Abu Aziz, God and he, Bayazid, God and all of mankind, are One. Bayazid realized that this Unity lay beyond the world of the senses, and that he now had to march steadfastly in that direction.

As soon as he resolved to do what Abu Aziz requested of him, Bayazid felt himself melting down to a wave of light undulating toward a brilliant ocean into which he merged and lost himself. He arose from this ocean like a liquid luminescence in the body of a child that was at once very old and very new. When he opened his eyes they were new eyes that could see beyond appearances of things into their Reality.

Bayazid tore out his dirhams from the lining of his robe, placed them before Abu Aziz, circled him seven times with the greatest reverence in his heart, and kissed him. When he left the next morning, after having shared their meager meal of dates and goat milk, Bayazid took Abu Aziz's words and put them in his ear, more resplendent than a golden earring studded with gems. ✿

# Bayazid's Holy Body

MATHNAWI, IV, 2102-2144

ANY OF BAYAZID'S disciples came to visit him every evening and stayed late into the night. In the early evenings they found him coherent and sane, but at night he would often go into ecstatic trances, withdraw into his own world and say things they couldn't understand or accept.

Every evening his disciples would ask him questions about spiritual matters and Bayazid's life, and the master would answer them.

"What is the best virtue for a human to posses?" one disciple asked one day. And Bayazid replied, "God-given good nature."

"What if a person doesn't have it?"

"Then health," Bayazid said. "If he doesn't have health, the best quality is to have ears that can hear the divine message, and eyes that can see beauty and divinity everywhere. If he doesn't have these, then a learned heart."

"What if he doesn't have any of these?"

"Then he's better off dead!" Bayazid laughed.

Another disciple asked, "I have done everything that I possibly could. I am disciplined about my prayers and meditation. I fast regularly. I sing Allah's praises, but I am no closer to Him than before."

"I know," Bayazid responded. "Hundreds of thousands are pious, like you. I too, once asked Allah: 'Why am I not closer to you? Why am I not more pious? Why don't I pray more?' And Allah replied, 'I have too much of piety and prayers. Give me something I do not have.' And I replied, 'I offer you my need, my longing, and my broken heart, O Allah!'"

"How long does it take to get enlightened?" another asked. The evening had worn on, and Bayazid was drifting towards a drunken rapture where his disciples couldn't follow.

"It takes many centuries for a flower such as me to grow in the garden of the universe. It's all about love, love, love," he said, falling into an ecstatic swoon.

Bayazid fell silent, his face began to glow with a mystical light, and soon a stream of tears was flowing down his face and into his beard. His disciples knew that now their master had entered a country where they couldn't follow.

The next evening, Bayazid started in his usual way.

"How old are you?" a disciple asked.

"Four," replied the master. His disciples thought he had lost his mind. "Up until four years ago, the mystery was veiled from me and I lived in a fog of ignorance and unknowing. Four years ago when I met my master, Abu Aziz, the veil lifted and I came into the world like a child."

"How did you become such a great Sufi?" another devotee asked.

"Through a woman," replied Bayazid. All his disciples were very shocked. A woman! She wasn't even worth half a man! Was Bayazid already slipping into irrationality?

"For years I went around searching for Sufi masters, purifying myself with pilgrimages, mortifying my body by fasting and prayers, but nothing worked. I went to the pious and got nothing from them. I went to the warriors and the mullahs and got nothing again. I asked Allah, and he said, 'Leave your self and come.' But I did not know how to go till one night my mother awoke me from sleep, asking for some water. I looked in the jar and I looked in the bucket, but there was no water in the house. It was a dark, moonless night, and I stumbled my way to the spring and fetched some. When I returned with the water, my mother was asleep, so I stayed awake and waited till she awoke at dawn. She was very surprised to see me sitting at her bedside in the morning. When she heard I had stayed up the whole night she was very surprised. She sat up, drank the water, then shut her eyes and prayed for me for hours. That morning I found the direction I had to go."

After answering several questions in a logical way, Bayazid again fell into a trance.

"O God," he cried, falling into a swoon. "How long will this barrier of 'and' remain between you and me? Take away this *I* from me! Take it away now, so only you remain. When I am with you, I am greater than all. When I am away from you, I am nothing, nothing, nothing!"

He was silent a long time, and then Bayazid's lips opened, and quietly at first, but growing louder, came the words: "There is no distinction between God and me. Lo, I am God. There is no God but me, so worship me!"

His disciples were dumbfounded with this blasphemy. They sat with their master till dawn, and when his drunken ecstasy passed, they said to him, "Master! You said something last night that really upset and angered us. You said you were God and that we were to worship you. This is impiety . . . blasphemy!"

"I did?" Bayazid asked, shocked. "This is indeed blasphemous. How can a mere human, so stuffed with sins and darkness, turmoil and burning, be God? I am mortal, tied to this body and these senses, and God transcends the body. Bring knives and daggers with you tomorrow. If I say anything like this ever again, slay me."

But the next night, the same thing happened again. Enraptured, he said, "In my body there is nothing but God . . . God in my fingers, God in my hair, God in my eyes and mouth and nose, God in my head, God in my heart, God in every atom of me! Do not seek elsewhere; God is here, here, here!"

Obedient to his command and in the hopes of saving their master from damnation, some of them brought out their knives and swords and lunged at Bayazid's holy body. But wonder of wonders! Every time a disciple plunged his knife into Bayazid, he found he had made a gash in his own body. Whoever went for the master's throat, found his own throat cut and bleeding. Whoever inflicted a blow on Bayazid's breast saw his own chest wounded. While all around him his over-zealous disciples fell bleeding and wounded, there was not even a mark or a scratch on Bayazid's body, which became empty as a mirror in which the disciples battled with their own reflections. Bayazid had emptied himself into the shining ocean of God like a river of light, and was safe from all harm. ֍

# VI

# Tame Your Ego

*Here self-effacement*
*is needed, not grammar.*
*If you are dead to self,*
*plunge into the sea*
*without peril!*

MATHNAWI, I, 2841

◇╫───⚬───╫◇

*You may know all*
*the minutiae of knowledge,*
*O scholar, but not by that means*
*will your inward eyes*
*that see the invisible*
*be opened.*

MATHNAWI, VI, 261

# Nouns and Verbs

MATHNAWI, I, 2835-2850

BDULLAH WAS A GREAT grammarian with a worldwide reputation and many scholarly disciples and admirers. He was a specialist in all the ways of words: morphology, morpho-phonemics, phonemics, phonetics, semiotics, semantics, phonology, etymology, and semasiology. He had a deep and impressive knowledge about the origins, history, mechanics of languages, and the meanings of language forms. Abdullah also believed that such knowledge was essential to the evolution of human beings to raise them far above the ignorant and language-deprived beasts. He had a theory, which he proved with overwhelming data and facts, that it was knowledge and awareness of language that accounted for success in all the spheres of life. Without it, humans too, were no better than animals.

"Take that boatman, for instance. Just look at him," Abdullah said to his coterie of disciples and admirers who had come to bid him goodbye on the shores of the swift and wide flowing river.

They looked and saw a shabby-looking man sitting in the stern of a boat. By him sat a monkey scratching his armpits and looking at them with an impassive face, his jaw jutting out beneath sad, beady eyes.

"He probably knows nothing about the rules of grammar and uses language only and entirely for the sake of a very rudimentary communication, like his brainless monkey. You!" Abdullah cried out aloud to the boatman.

"Sahib?" returned the boatman. His cloak was torn and patched, and his turban in rags. "Boat . . . ready . . . come!"

"See?" said Abdullah to his students. "He speaks in fragments, and not merely in fragments but in disjointed words that barely convey his thought. If he had said, 'Yes, Sahib, my boat is ready and waiting for you,' he would be a man of a different . . . species, almost. But then, if he knew how to speak well, like a human being, he wouldn't be a boatman, but a Sahib himself."

His disciples laughed.

"And if you ask him why he is so ragged, he will tell you he believes in spiritual poverty. These *fakirs* (holy men) would rather spend their time meditating and praying. They talk little and save all their energies for spiritual advancement. Spiritual poverty! It is the rationalization of poor and miserable people who won't take the trouble to study language and improve their lot!" Abdullah spat with disgust. "Listen to this. 'Do you know anything about grammar?'" he shouted to the boatman over the roar of the river.

"Gra . . . maa? What is . . .?"

"What an ass, or rather, what a monkey!" Abdullah said to his disciples, who were learning from him how to do their own research, and who were busy taking down the words of their master so they, too, could become masters themselves, or at least write a biography of their adulated master.

"He doesn't know what grammar is, let alone anything about its glories! How can people be so unaware and stupid?" said Abdullah's favorite student, who had not only imbibed the language, but also the temperament of his master.

Nearing the boat, Abdullah said to the boatman. "Man, you don't you even know what grammar is? What kind of a life is it when you don't even know what grammar is, leave alone its magnificence? Without it, you have wasted half your life."

Abdullah stepped into the boat and it rocked. For a moment he lost his footing and almost fell overboard. He had a moment of terror, but he steadied himself with the thought of his accomplishments. Grammar, after all, as he knew and lectured about it, was the only certainty and security in life, and was an indication of the supreme meaning and syntax of the world. It always saved him in moments of doubt. Settling down in the small plank in the aft, away from the monkey who had begun to howl for some strange reason, crying and cackling, Abdullah smiled inwardly. The boat was so small it couldn't contain all the tomes he had written on grammar and language. Abdullah smiled and waved at the students who were waving and bowing deferentially as they bid him a tearful goodbye.

Silently, the boatman pushed off with his paddle and began to row the boat to the middle of the river.

"Stop that monkey from making those horrible noises!" Abdullah shouted at the boatman. "Dumb animal! Why is he so agitated?"

"Storm . . . coming," the boatman said.

Abdullah was so busy waving to his admirers and mulling over the success of his last lecture, that he didn't notice that suddenly a gale had sprung up and a fierce wind had started to blow, roiling the water and causing big waves. The boat began to swirl and toss in the storm, and in the blink of an eye it had half capsized into the river.

"Know . . . swim?" asked the boatman as he calmly watched the grammarian lurch from side to side, his face in a disturbed and fearful grimace. No nouns or verbs came to the grammarian's rescue as he faced his own inevitable end.

"No," was all that he could manage to say before he was flung out of the boat and into the roiling waters.

"Oh," cried the boatman, as the boat broke in half, and the paddle was wrenched out of his hand. "Sahib's whole life . . . wasted!"

The boatman and the monkey, with strong and certain

strokes of their arms, reached the shore. Wet and shivering, and holding each other for warmth, they sat upon the banks and watched with compassion the sight of the great grammarian Sahib drowning. ৯

# The Company You Keep

MATHNAWI, II, 1932-2035; 2064-2094; 2124-2130

AFIQ, A SUFI, prided himself on being a hero. Like a doctor who seeks pain and disease to cure, Rafiq sought to save helpless beings. Wherever and whenever anyone was in distress, Rafiq went to rescue him, no matter what the risk to his own life. Well, he didn't consider it too much of a risk because he had special powers, much courage, and a resolute fearlessness that served him well. In time, Rafiq developed quite a reputation for being a hero, which he enjoyed thoroughly. His only regret in life was that he didn't have as large a following as he would have liked. Well, he did have a few admirers, but because of his peregrinating lifestyle, he frequently found himself all alone in the desert. He wished he had somebody who would serve and adore him all the time.

One day while Rafiq was resting under the shade of a palm tree, he was aroused by desperate cries. A ferocious, scaly dragon was about to swallow a big, black, wild and wooly bear, which was roaring and screaming for help.

Rafiq ran to the rescue of the bear whose head was already in the dragon's mouth while his legs waved in the air frantically. Fearlessly, Rafiq grabbed the bear's legs, stared at the dragon to hypnotize him with his powerful gaze, and with all his might, pulled the bear out of his mouth. The dazed bear rubbed his head as the dragon slunk away like a frightened mouse.

Rafiq congratulated himself at his success at the rescue. He lived for experiences like these, which called for his compassion and affirmed his own loving kindness. The bear, realizing that this man had saved him, fell at Rafiq's feet in gratitude and followed him wherever he went. When Rafiq lay down to sleep, the bear stood guard over him; when Rafiq was hungry, the bear hunted and fetched him food; when Rafiq grew thirsty, the bear would find water and carry it in the cup of his palms for his master.

One day a sage passed by and saw Rafiq asleep with the bear beside him. The sage shook him up, and shouted: "Wake up! Wake up! There is a bear by your side!"

"I know," Rafiq said, and recounted the story of how he had rescued the bear, adding many heroic details to the original rescue. Rafiq liked to recount his exploits with an audience. It made him see himself through others' eyes, and loved what he saw.

"You have done a good deed, but now get away from him. The friendship of a fool is worse than his enmity," the sage said.

"But he has attached himself to me and makes me feel like a king," Rafiq replied.

"Your heroism has gone to your head, which is swollen and intoxicated with the desire to be desired. Drive him away by all means!"

"Why should I? He is a great companion. Look how he's chasing away flies that want to land on me. Look at his affection for me." The bear lovingly put his arm around Rafiq, and licked his face, gently.

"His flattery is a sweet morsel. Do not eat it! It is a burning coal! The affection of fools is flattering to the ego. It swells one's head, but in the end it is dangerous," the sage said.

"You are just jealous that you don't have a bear of your own to serve you in your journeys," Rafiq laughed.

"Better to be alone on this journey than be with something that is not like-minded. I tremble with anxiety for you. Don't go into the forest with a companion such as this. Beware! Beware!"

But Rafiq's ears were deaf to his words. By pulling the bear out of the dragon's jaws, he had in fact given it life, as a mother would her infant. He found this simile especially pleasing, for it put him in the role of a creator and preserver.

"Since your ears are plugged with your ego, and your brain is deaf to my words, I leave you to your fate," the sage said.

"You have interrupted my sleep. Go away and stop meddling in my affairs. No bear would attach himself and serve you, you coward!" The sage moved on.

The sun had climbed up in the sky, and the day became hot. Rafiq crawled into the bear's shade and slept. The air was loud with flies, buzzing and ringing in the bear's and Rafiq's ears and eyes. The bear kept driving the flies away, but despite his frantic efforts, they kept landing on Rafiq's face. Angry at the flies for bothering him and disturbing the sleep of the one he worshiped, the bear picked up a rock. In his zeal to protect his master from this annoyance, he flung the rock at the flies, crushing Rafiq's skull to smithereens. ♠

# A Dead Ass

*MATHNAWI*, II, 156-264

HALID GREW WEARY in his travels around the world, lecturing and discoursing on important spiritual issues, and decided to take a rest at a monastery for Sufis. When he rode up to the gate, he was informed that a conference was in progress on various mystical matters. When Khalid told them he was a Sufi himself, they invited him to participate and deliver a lecture on any subject of his choice.

"I could give my lecture on taming the ego," he thought. "That always goes over well. 'More invisible than the footprints of an ant on a black rock on the darkest night of the year are the workings of the ego.' What a marvelous quote," he mused. "I wish I could remember who said that. I would definitely like to credit the author, for I am a scholar and do not like to borrow other people's ideas without citing them. Oh, well. I shall quote it anyway and humbly admit that I do not know. "

Deep in thought, Khalid alighted from his ass and led it to the stable. He noticed his ass looked weak and feeble from her travels. Khalid wondered if he had worked her too hard. She had aged in his service. As he patted her rump, he realized in a flash what the subject of his new lecture would be: animals and the need for compassion towards them. The Sufi's business was love, and it had to be expressed toward all God's creatures without discrimination. "And," he thought, his mind quickening, "I will connect this subject to the idea of the need to pay as much attention to the practical aspects of life, like taking care of your animals, as to contemplation."

Khalid wanted to tend to his old donkey, but handing her over to one of the servants and enjoining him to take good care of her, he walked to and fro, preparing his lecture. Having done so, he enthusiastically joined his fellow Sufis who were talking about all sorts of sacred issues: the need to meditate, pray, read from sacred texts, the importance of explications and analysis of the Koran, and other fine points of spirituality. Khalid also gave his discourse, to much applause.

In a break in the conference, a feast was brought in, and Khalid wondered if his ass had been fed. Before partaking of the feast, he motioned to the servant he had handed his animal to, and said: "Go into the stable and feed my ass straw and barley, but please make sure first that the barley is wet, since she is an old ass and her teeth are loose."

"I have already thought of that," the servant replied.

"And mix only a little bit of straw in the barley. She needs good nourishment in her old age."

"That is obvious," he said, obviously offended at being told how to conduct his business.

"Good! But would you please make sure her saddle is off. And here," Khalid said, producing a small container from his saddle bag, "put this salve on the sores on her back."

"Sir, we have salve in the stables!" the servant replied.

"And the water you give her, please let it be lukewarm. Cold water hurts her teeth and is bad for her digestion."

"Sir, I have been taking care of donkeys all my life!"

"Good. I am glad she is in such good hands. But please do clear her resting place of stones and dung, and if it is wet, put some dry earth or old sacks on it. Her joints are rheumatic."

"Sir, I always keep the stable clean and dry!"

"But, the stones in her shoes! You've . . ."

"Done!" the servant said, and turned away.

During this entire dialogue, the Sufis listened intently to Khalid's words. All of them had one thought in their heads: Khalid's ideas about the treatment of animals were deeply felt and implemented. He had meant every word he spoke. To take such good care of an old donkey! Indeed, this Sufi had arrived at love and compassion's gate. He was a role model to all of them.

Over dinner, the head Sufi invited Khalid to stay on in the monastery as their guest, but Khalid declined their generous offer. He was scheduled for some more lectures in his itinerary, and he needed to be on his way in the morning.

The Sufis gave Khalid their best bed. The sheets were clean, a jar of water lay by his bedside, a cool breeze blew in from the oasis through an open window, and the stars sparkled brightly in the desert air. What a luxury to have such comfort for his old bones! Giving thanks to God, Khalid undressed, got into bed, and fell asleep right away.

He had a very disturbing dream. A wolf was tearing off pieces of flesh from his donkey's back and thighs. She was staggering along, falling now into a well, and now into a ditch. Khalid tried to get up to go check on his ass, but fatigue got the better of him. The sheets were soft and sleep was heavy upon him. He consoled himself with the thought that it was just a dream, turned over, and fell asleep again.

Meanwhile, in the stables, Khalid's poor ass was in dire straights. The servant had simply taken her and tied her to a stake. With her saddle still askew and heavy upon her sore back, she was unable to settle down comfortably on the wet and stony earth. She had neither been fed nor watered. Tormented by hunger, thirst, pain, and discomfort, she tossed about all night, a bitter monologue repeating itself in her head.

"Too many journeys, too many places, too many burdens. Oh, why can't my master just stay still in one place and let me rest and feed in peace and comfort? Dear God, why do you give your animals so much pain and torment? Heavy loads, beatings, saddles on sore backs, shoes on weary, bleeding feet. Why in your world of abundance is there so much hunger and suffering for your animals? I cry my mournful song in the market place, but who hears me? They laugh or think, 'That's the way donkeys cry; there's nothing unusual in it.' But do they ever bother to ask why we cry like this? Generations of loads, Lord, have determined our howl. Even a bit of dry straw would do nicely now. I would chew it slowly and savor it, and be content. You can keep the barley and the sugar. My master is all talk. I have grown old in his service and he won't even retire me. What good am I retired? He still has to feed me, so he'll just ride me to death. What a prison this life is! O God, I have always borne your burdens willingly, for that lightened my load. But tonight I am weary, very weary. I want to return to you where there is no labor. I want to roam the meadows of paradise without burdens now. O let me graze slowly and lingeringly in your fields!"

The next day, in the morning when Khalid asked for his donkey, the servant went to the stable, gave the poor donkey a few blows with a goad, stood her up, straightened her saddle, and led her, limping, to Khalid and his bags. He had gained a lot of admirers in the monastery and was most pleased. They stood around him, sorry to see him go.

Khalid mounted the donkey, and she collapsed beneath him, sending Khalid face downward to the ground. Surprised and embarrassed, he dusted himself, lifted her up, and mounted her again. This time her legs gave way beneath her and Khalid was once again in the dirt.

One monk advised that Khalid twist the donkey's ears hard, another that he should whip her back into health since she was probably only lazy. How could a donkey that had been so well cared for and fed not be ready to do her master's bidding? Yet another thought she was tired because she had stayed awake all night remembering God.

But in his heart, Khalid knew the truth. The stable boy had not heeded his commands. He wanted to whip him, but that would reveal his carelessness in the matter to the admiring monks. Besides, the servant was nowhere to be found. Khalid knew that the fault was his own. His lecture about animals had been more important to him than his animal. He had been tripped up by his ego.

As Khalid stood around with the others, tears streaming down his face as he watched his beloved donkey breathing her last breath, he realized what an enormous mistake he had made. He should have checked on her himself. But, he thought, wiping his tears, there was so much to learn, so much to teach. He would humbly include this story in his next lecture. Perhaps the theme would be: "If you love something, don't leave its care to others," or, "do your own work unless you want a dead ass on your hands." No, better still, he would expand his lecture on the ego and include the incident in it. Oh how subtly and insidiously the ego works! "More invisible than the footprints of an ant . . ."

So Khalid bought himself a new donkey, young and strong, and as he rode him, kindly, lovingly, tending to each of his needs personally, he prepared the content of his next lecture. ⚘

# The Dangers of Imitation

MATHNAWI, II, 514-563

AVING LEARNED a bitter lesson in the earlier story about delegating responsibility to negligent servants, Khalid did not take any chances this time with his new ass. He had learned to do his own important work. After a great deal of traveling about, he arrived at a monastery and took his ass to the stable himself. There he cleared a patch of earth, patted down some soft burlap, took off his ass's saddle and saddlebags, put some balm on his sores, checked for and removed a few stones from his shoes, fed him some barley and straw and water, and even treated him to a lump of sugar from his sack. Having taken good care of his beast himself, he posted a stable boy outside the stall, and paid him well to ensure no harm came to his animal.

Khalid noticed that the monastery looked dilapidated. Some walls were crumbling and the windows were broken. When the Sufi monks came to greet him, they looked emaciated and feeble, and their clothes were worn so thin they were falling off their backs. In a flash, the subject of Khalid's next lecture came to him. There was a disturbing trend in Sufi circles of taking the idea of spiritual poverty to an extreme. They did not make the fine, but imperative, distinction between working in the world, earning a living, and being meek and humble. Khalid knew that the two were not incompatible. He himself worked hard at his lectures and made a living off of them. These ragged Sufis, too, were, no doubt blindly imitating the fad. Khalid would discourse on the necessity of being in touch with one's own, inner needs, taking responsibility for one's own life instead of being swept away by someone else's lifestyle.

"But how shall I tie all this in with my excellent lecture on the ego?" he wondered. Deep in thought, he walked to and fro. "The ego works in subtle ways and has many forms," he thought. "People imitate others because the ego is afraid to be left out, to feel separate, and to go against the grain of mass trends, even if the mass trend is towards laziness, self-denial, poverty, and starvation! Oh, how devious the ego can be! One has to be constantly on guard against it."

Khalid felt sorry for them and discoursed late into the night in an empty, dark room. The Sufis were too poor to buy candles. Khalid talked at length about the dangers inherent in imitation. Poverty, he said, can often bring the soul to perdition. It can bring the body to such sore need that everything becomes fair game, and many a dishonest act appears, mistakenly, to be a virtuous one.

Khalid was hungry, and wished there was some food. His hunger gave fire to his lecture about taking care of the body. Just when he could carry on no more, delicious aromas wafted to his nostrils. God, in confirmation of the truth of his sayings, was sending provender!

The Sufis' nostrils flared and their spirits lifted.

"I smell roasted goat!" one cried.

"And rice," said another.

"Vegetables!" said a third.

"Ah, and syrupy sweetmeats!" Khalid said. "The angels are providing! God is very generous to us today. Keep my message in mind, work hard, and you shall want for nothing, brothers."

The poor Sufis rejoiced. They were done with beggary and patience and fasting, and eating the light of God. They wanted food!

"Oh Sufi," they cried, looking at Khalid with adoration and gratitude. "You have entered our monastery tonight, put your feet in our humble abode, and God has provided for us!"

Khalid believed them. Yes, he was definitely arriving at the end of the Way. God was pleased with him and his humility in acknowledging his shortcomings.

One of the Sufis brought in some candles, wine, and snacks. Khalid, wearied from his travels and his lectures, wanted to make merry tonight. To hell with all his lectures! To hell with thought and eternal vigilance against the ego! Tonight it was time to drink and dance.

He filled the cups all around and they caroused. An entire banquet of delicacies was soon served. Everybody ate their fill, licking their fingers and smacking their lips. When they were done, musicians arrived to sing divine songs to which the Sufis could dance.

As they began their *sama*, the mystical dance, the monastery was filled with sounds of revelry, and everyone was in a state of ecstasy. Now that God had filled their stomachs, they waved their hands, beat the ground with their feet, whirled about, and went into ecstasy.

When the sama had run its course from beginning to end, and the tired and inebriated Sufis sank to the floor to rest, the minstrel struck up a catchy tune, and began to sing, in its various permutations, the strain of "the ass is gone, the ass is gone."

The tired Sufis, energized once more, began to sing along, "The ass is gone, the ass is gone." The entire company shared in the enthusiasm, including Khalid. Soon, they were up again, clapping their hands, stamping their feet, and singing at the top of their voices, "the ass is gone, the ass is gone." Khalid had not had such a good time in a while. These Sufis knew how to live, and he was happy to be following their example. Scholarship and lecturing were hard work and for a while he felt released into insouciance. The revelry went on all night, and only stopped in the wee hours of the morning, when all of them lay in a heap on the floor, and fell asleep, snoring.

Khalid awoke with a start and a headache. The room was empty, the Sufis were gone, and the sun was high in the sky. It was time for him to leave and begin his travels. He cleaned his saddlebags and brought them out to tie them on his ass. He went into the stable, but did not find his ass.

"The stable boy must be watering him," Khalid thought, "because when I fed him last night, he took very little water." Soon the stable boy arrived, rubbing his eyes, and the ass was not with him.

"Where is my ass?" Khalid asked, beginning to get anxious and angry.

"Don't ask me such a foolish question," the stable boy replied.

"I entrusted the ass to you. Where is he? I demand to know! I'll take you to the Cadi!"

"You threw a liver to a hundred hungry cats and then wonder what happened to it?"

"What do you mean?" Khalid asked.

"The ass is gone," the stable boy replied, winking at Khalid, and twirling around.

"Where? Why didn't you come and tell me?" Khalid fumed. "I posted you outside the stable to make sure he was safe! I paid you to do that!"

"I came many times to tell you but you were always singing 'the ass is gone, the ass is gone' with such fervor that I thought you knew that they sold your ass to buy food and pay the musicians."

"Oh!" cried Khalid, lifting his hand to strike the boy. "Didn't you know that I delighted in singing along with them because they were singing so merrily?"

"How could I know?" the boy replied, getting ready to strike back. "I thought to myself as you sang with the others, 'Here is a man who is aware and content with God's judgment.' How did I know you were only imitating the others?" ⚘

# Spend! Spend! Spend!

*MATHNAWI, V, 477-498*

ARAD WAS A HAPPY, joyous man who roamed from town to town. He owned nothing but the clothes on his back and tattered shoes that were adequate for his travels. He knew that when they fell apart, Allah would provide him with a pair of old shoes that would do. They may be a bit too big, or a tiny bit too small, but good enough to protect his feet. Once a stranger had even taken Farad to a shop and bought him a pair of shining new shoes that fit very well! Sometimes he had to go without food, or make do with only a crust, but never for too long because there were always kind people who fed him enough to keep him healthy and happy. Didn't the mullah of his mosque always tell him to trust in Allah? Farad's trust was never betrayed. When you throw yourself on Allah's mercy, He provides.

Because Farad's faith had relieved him of struggle and worry, he spent all of his time adoring Allah, being happy, and singing his joy at the top of his lungs.

One day, skipping down the street of a town far from his own village, merrily singing a song, Farad heard the sound of crying and lamenting. He turned the corner and there, kneeling over his dog, was the mullah from his village, weeping loudly. The dog looked very thin and emaciated, his ribs showing through the thin upholstery of his skin. He was breathing his last breath.

"What happened?" Farad asked the mullah to whom he owed so much of his faith and joy.

"My dog," sobbed the mullah. "He's dying! I loved him so much! He was such a faithful companion—he loved me when I was alone, hunted for me, caught prey for my food, watched over me at night."

"Is he sick? Did someone harm him?"

"Hunger," replied the mullah. "He is dying of hunger! No, look, he's dead. He has breathed his last!"

"But . . . how can that be?" Farad asked, confused about how the mullah's dog could die of starvation. The mullah, thanks to contributions by his congregation, was well off. Seeing a fat bag lying by the mullah, the he asked, "What's in this?"

"My food bag," replied the mullah, tears streaming down his face.

"But why didn't you give some morsels to your dog?" The dumbfounded man asked.

"I'm going for Hajj, and Mecca is a long way from here. I will need all this food for the journey."

"Oh mullah, you are nothing but a water-skin full of wind! You do not live your sermons!"

"Sermons are all very well, but one has to be practical. What will I eat when there isn't any left? If I don't provide for myself, who will?"

"God, O fool, God! It is your ego that keeps you from trusting! It is your ego that keeps you from love! It is your ego that worries about the future! Let go your ego that makes you constantly struggle and fear, and God *will* provide. You taught me to tame my ego but couldn't tame your own. Despite knowing the truth, you have chosen your ego over trust, a crust of bread over the feast of love! Do not hoard up the purse of your service, but give everything for love! God tells us: Spend! Spend! Spend! Hold nothing back! Rush into the fire of love like a moth, O ignorant mullah!" ✿

# VII

# Be Humble

*How can a rock*
*become green*
*in spring*

*and grow flowers?*

*For years*
*you have been*
*a heart—tearing rock:*

*now, once*
*for the sake of*
*experiment, be earth!*

*MATHNAWI*, I, 1911

# The Roar in the Mirror

*MATHNAWI*, I, 900-1372

HE ANIMALS OF a valley in the jungle were very troubled by a violent, arrogant, and destructive lion. He often killed other animals just for the sport of it. He had defeated all the other lions in the jungle, had no competition from anyone, and reveled in his strength and power.

The animals—the fox and deer, hare and jackal—had no peace of mind, and lived in constant fear of the lion's ambushes and senseless carnage. He would carry off their young, eat one or two, and use the others as bait to attract other animals that he also killed and left lying around his lair, to show off his power and his unmatchable hunting skills. In their desperation the animals decided to send a delegation to the lion and propose a compromise.

The lion saw them coming and was about to swoop on them all when a little hare with perky ears, bright round eyes, and a dark nose spoke up with a surprisingly loud voice. It was his idea to bring the delegation to the lion.

"Wait, king of beasts, wait! We have come to you with a proposal that will make you very comfortable and happy."

"I am very comfortable and very happy already," the lion smirked, sharpening his claws on the bark of a tree.

"Our plan . . . will keep you well fed in your old age, Sire."

"Old age?" The lion smiled, contemplating his beautiful, healthy claws, sharp like sabers. "Who's old?"

"You're not at all old, your majesty. All around us is evidence of your youth and your vigor. I only meant that our solution will ensure that you will be provided for down the road—when you grow old and are incapable of hunting," the hare said with a deep bow.

"Grow old and incapable of hunting?" the lion laughed with a growl. "Don't fool yourselves. I will never grow old!" But it just so happened that the lion had himself been thinking a bit about aging. Lately, his fur was getting a little ragged, his joints had lost a bit of their agility, his vitality was flagging, and his heart beat altogether too loudly when he exerted himself. Images of scraggly predecessors, fathers and grandfathers, their manes and tails mangy and flea-infested, their bodies scrawny and weak, flashed through his mind. How they had slunk out of the forest, wounded and bleeding after his fight with them for supremacy! What if a stronger, younger lion strayed into his territory in the future and did the same to him? A nagging fear had taken hold of him, and though externally fierce and loud, he allowed the hare to carry on.

"Well, morsel? What did you have in mind?"

"We will ensure that you get a daily, fixed allowance of meat. We will draw lots and one of us will come to you every morning, and you can feast on us to your fill. But in return you have to promise us that you won't hunt anyone else, and leave us in peace. This valley, O mighty lion, has become bitter to us, and we would like to rest a while, and replenish and fatten ourselves . . . for you, of course."

Though the lion was disappointed that this deal wouldn't allow him to kill for fun—though he resolved silently to do what he liked without any restraints if he felt like it—after daylong negotiations and discussions, he agreed to a trial of the proposal. He threatened to change the rules if the arrangement didn't work for him.

"Make sure that my food arrives on time each day. I don't like to be kept waiting when I am hungry. Even a moment's delay will break our covenant," the lion said.

"So be it," the animals agreed.

So it was that every day one animal, to whose lot it fell to be the lion's meal for the day, hurried to the lion, resigned to the will of God and destiny.

When it was the hare's turn, he did not want to go. He had just found a lovely mate and was so blissfully in love with her and all of life, so eager to begin a family and live in joy that he cried out: "I won't go! For how long shall we suffer this injustice?"

The animals became very angry with him for his rebellion and for jeopardizing their contract and their peace. "We have sacrificed ourselves for the good of all, and now do not give us a bad name or betray our honor. Do not anger the lion! Go, go quickly to him, or you will be late!"

The hare replied, "Let me get rid of the lion."

"Who do you think you are, you tiny little nothing, to jeopardize our peace?"

"You are just a hare! Recognize it, and live within your limits. Stop this ridiculous bragging! A hare rescue us from the lion!"

"My friends, everything is possible with the help of God," replied the hare.

Some animals called him proud, some mad and crazy, but some of them longed in their heart to be freed from the noose of death, and a few believed the hare was a prophet for even thinking such a release possible.

"I may be a weak and small hare, but God has sent me an idea and an inspiration. If God so wills, even a weakling can become strong, for strength comes from the mind to the body. If you make an alliance with God, then the entire universe comes to your aid. I cannot fail."

"Tell us what your plan is, and we will advise you on it."

"I will reveal it to none. If you breathe a secret even to a mirror, it loses its clarity," the hare replied.

"Please, let me come with you!" pleaded his mate.

"Yes, of course," the others responded. "Go, for the lion will be angry if we send him just one measly little hare. The addition of your mate will placate him."

"No, my beloved," the hare said. "Stay back and fatten yourself. I will return and we will start our family. But I must make our world safe for our offspring. And you, my dear mate, will be with me in spirit in my story and my plan."

"What story, what plan?" cried some. "Tell us!"

"Shut up and let him leave quickly," said others. "Hurry up! Hurry up! You are getting late!"

"I'll tell you this much. Being late is part of my plan," the hare said, hopping away in a slow and deliberate manner. On the way he tarried here and there, and even took a nice long nap under the shade of a tree. When he arrived at the lion's lair, the lion was in a raging fury, as the hare had hoped. He was tearing up the ground and flinging the skeletons of the dead animals into the air.

"Didn't I say," he snarled, "didn't I know that you were all villains? Dishonorable! Liars! The contract is broken! I will devour all of you now! I will slaughter your young and eat their juicy organs and drink their blood! I will spare no one . . . none . . . not a bird shall remain, I will do such things, I will . . ."

The hare had been trying to say something, but the lion was so enraged that he couldn't get beyond ". . . listen . . . but . . . hear me . . . if you will only . . . please . . . your majesty."

"These claws, the sabers of my teeth, these muscles have brought down elephants, whole hordes of them, do you hear me? I have mounted the backs of the biggest and strongest oxen and sucked the hot, warm blood from their jugular veins, then torn them limb from limb while they still breathed. I ate their organs—livers, heart, brain. Heart and brains and eyeballs are my favorite. Who do you think you are? And what do they mean by sending me—late! Late! Our covenant is off, off, off! One, just one tiny, puny little tit-bit, a hare with the heart and brain the size of a pea, of a seed! Oh! How I was in the mood for brain and heart today. Serves me right for trusting these stupid, dishonest animals!"

"I have an excuse, sir," the hare said when the lion had quieted down a bit.

"What excuse could you have, you rat? You will get stuck between my teeth like a particle, and that is to be my breakfast?"

"When I set out this morning, on time, your highness, my mate was with me, plump and fat, ready and happy to sacrifice herself for you. But on the way, a young lion attacked and captured us. I said to him, 'We are slaves of the King of the Jungle, he is waiting for us, please, please let us go.' He laughed aloud when I mentioned you, and especially laughed derisively when I called you the King of the Jungle, and called you that 'old bit of rotten meat.' I pleaded with him to let us see your face for the last time and carry the news to you. I promised to bring him more animals in the afternoon, made a deal with him, and he let me come to you. But he made me leave my mate behind as a hostage. I have come to tell you that the thread of our promise is broken. The other lion has taken your meal and my mate, and I can do nothing, nothing," the hare wept.

The lion's wrath knew no bounds. Another lion in *his* territory? Eating *his* meal? Evil . . . monstrous . . . wicked . . . vicious . . .

Words failed him and he sat on his haunches, howling and sputtering with rage.

"If you want your daily allowance, there is only one way, sire. Get rid of the other one. You can do it, your majesty, for you are strong and . . ."

"Of course I can. Don't tell me what I can do, you . . . crumb!" the lion lashed out, itching to tear the poor hare into shreds, but controlled himself, knowing he needed the hare to lead him to the other lion.

"Take me to this . . . imposter!" he spat.

With the hare leading the way, they walked many miles to a well. As they approached the well, the hare fell back, as if terrified and afraid.

"Why are you lagging, you scrap?" the lion said, beginning to get very infuriated. They had traveled a while, and there was no lion in sight. "And where in the devil's name is that lion?"

"He . . . lives in the well, your majesty," the hare said, quavering with fear. "This is his fortress, and he is holding my companion, your breakfast, captive in it."

With the hare by his side, the lion walked to the well. With a loud growl that resounded far and wide, he looked inside. In the clear, circular mirror of the still waters of the well, he saw a lion roaring back a challenge to him, and beside him the rest of his meal—a plump hare, staring back with frightened eyes.

The lion shouted: "That hare is *my* meal, you son of a donkey!" And when the lion in the well echoed his words, matching his own fury, the lion, mad and blinded by rage, leaped into the well.

As the lion made a big splash, and thrashed about in the waters before drowning, the hare shouted to him: "The aggression that you see in others is your own nature reflected in them, O lion."

The hare jumped and danced, hopped, skipped, and leaped joyously all the way back to the meadow. In his heart was a song of gratitude and joy. He had delivered his brethren, and himself, from their daily dose of death.

In the meadow, the animals waiting anxiously for the outcome of the day saw the hare coming out of the thicket, leaping in the air and bounding towards them. They were thrilled at the sight. They crowded around him when he reached them, and his mate rushed to his side in relief. He told them the story of how they were free of the lion, and there was great rejoicing and laughter, dancing and singing. They formed a ring around the hare and his mate, and sang a song of praise to him as they danced in the light of the stars.

"Stop! Stop!" the hare cried, stopping suddenly. "My brothers and sisters, don't praise me. Praise the power that made this brain. Without this power I would be journeying through the guts of the lion even now. Who was I, a little pea-brained, pimple-hearted hare, to accomplish this huge task on my own?"

And when the thanksgiving was made, hand in hand the hare and his mate hopped into their burrow to start their family, fearlessly. 🙝

# Ayaz's Secret Treasure

MATHNAWI, V, 1857-2149; 3251-3355; 3635-3643; 3707-3715

ING MAHMOUD OF Ghazni loved his slave, Ayaz, as dearly as his own life. Ayaz, he knew, was loving, loyal, and an enthusiastic supporter. Ayaz's joy in life lay in service, and the king rewarded him handsomely for it. Though he came from humble beginnings, Ayaz, on account of the king's generosity, acquired a great deal of wealth and influence over the years. He owned property, mansions and farms, horses and carriages. Because the king took personal interest in Ayaz's appearance and presented him with expensive outfits, Ayaz dressed in the finest robes made of silk and rare wools from Kashmir, the *pasham*, and the *shah toosh*. Even his shoes, made of the softest leather, were embroidered by the best of seamstresses with threads of beaten gold and silver, precious gems from the best mines of the earth, emeralds and rubies, pearls and sapphires.

Ayaz's fellow slaves and even the officials were very jealous of him. The emir, especially, was consumed with dislike of this upstart who, for no reason except a sycophantic obedience to the commands of the king, had become his favorite.

"Ayaz has so much power over the king that the king is *his* slave!" the emir said at a conference of all Ayaz's rivals. "The king is blinded by his love for him and thinks Ayaz is perfect and pure. He can't see what I can see so clearly. Though Ayaz may appear to be a wise and humble man, Ayaz's essence is evil. Why should he appear to be so obedient if not to gain the king's trust, and then plot his downfall, if not assassination? Our king is now the sultan of a large empire that includes all of Afghanistan, Iran, and all of North West India. Ayaz wants to dethrone him and become the sultan himself!"

"Yes!" cried the others, finding their own, secret thoughts reflected in the emir's words. "But the king loves him so much he won't hear a word against him. Let's find some proof of his disloyalty so the king will believe us!"

"Every man has a secret that he lets no one else see, and we will find his!"

"I know his! I know his!" a soldier shouted. "Almost every night, under the cover of darkness, Ayaz steals out of his house disguised in ordinary clothes, almost like a beggar, and visits one of his mansions. He disappears in it for hours on end, sometimes only emerging before the darkness begins to give way to day. "

"He's secretly depraved! Wine and women, many of them!" said one official.

"Young boys," said another.

"He's hatching a plot to overthrow the king!" the emir said. So each surmised, according to his own desire.

"Can't be," said a third, who prided himself on his reasoning. "He always looks fresh and in good health to be a debauch. Even if is he was hatching a plot he would be up all night wracking his brain. There must be some other explanation."

"You're right," said the soldier. "Besides, I have never seen any sign of life in that mansion. No women, no men, no boys, not even a guard outside, no lights, no noise, just silence.

"After unlocking seven locks on heavy bolts upon the front door, he enters and shuts it. Shortly after that, I can hear each of the seven bolts from the inside being drawn and locked. I was close behind him one day and caught a glimpse of another chamber inside that had a door with seven locks on it! I put my ear to the wall outside and heard him repeat the process seven times! He has such an intimate secret that he keeps it locked away inside seven chambers! His mansion is so heavily fortified that there can be only one reason for his precautions. Being the king's favorite, he is also in charge of the treasury. He is stealing gold, gems, and stashing them away!"

"The king's favorite . . . a common thief!" they cried. "Wait till the king discovers this!"

"But do you see him carrying sacks on his back when he enters?" one considered.

"No," said the soldier.

"But what does that mean? How many rare gems does it take to fill a pocket?" The emir said.

"Even a pocket full of gold is a lot!"

"Yes, why else would he go there every night? A pocket full of gold and gems every night for so many years . . . we have it! We have it!"

Early the next day, Ayaz's rivals requested a private audience with the king.

"We have come with some . . . sad news, your highness. We would rather not be the ones to give it to you, but our loyalty to you will not let us keep silent," the emir said, looking as sorrowful as he could. And then he proceeded to tell the king what he had discovered, together with his certainty of the only possible explanation for Ayaz's strange behavior.

There was a long silence in which the king seemed to be vacillating between his unshakable trust in Ayaz and doubt in him based upon this new knowledge. And then, as if the doubt had won out, he stood up from his throne and hopped and danced about in utter rage.

"What does he mean by concealing anything from me? I have treated him so well, and he steals from me! Hypocrite! He professes loyalty and love only to mask his true nature!"

"We seek your permission, your majesty, to tear down the doors and see what he is concealing!"

"Yes, yes, go," said the king to the men after some deliberation. "Go in secret to Ayaz's mansion when he is not there, and leave no trace of your visit. I don't want him to be hurt by our mistrust if we should find nothing. Discover his secret. If you find gold and gems, I will never see Ayaz's face again. Whatever you find is yours to keep. Distribute it amongst yourselves."

Shortly after midnight, when a spy informed the emir that Ayaz had locked the doors of the mansion behind him and retired to his home to sleep, the emir set out with thirty officers holding torches to visit Ayaz's secret chamber. All the way there they fantasized about the wealth they would acquire that night.

"After tonight our purses will be stuffed with gold!" one man whispered.

"Gold?" said another. "Think rather of precious gems! Have you seen how Ayaz lives? The clothes he wears, the shoes, the jewelry? I tell you, he has diamonds, emeralds, rubies as large as my nose stashed away in the chamber!"

"We, too, shall be lords after tonight!"

"We'll dress in silks and expensive wools, and own many homes!"

"We'll retire!"

They arrived, and proceeded to unscrew the bolts of all the doors, till finally they arrived at Ayaz's innermost chamber. Their torches revealed a room entirely empty except for some shabby looking clothes hanging near an alcove with an unlit but still soft and smoldering candle in it. A tattered and dirty sheepskin jacket patched up with bits of fabric in a hundred places hung above an altar on which lay a pair of dusty, battered old shoes full of holes. The soles were almost worn out and the dry, shriveled leather was fraying from too much use. A lute leaned against the wall on the floor.

"Check the pocket of this rag and tear open its lining!" the emir said after a long silence in which disappointment battled with a certainty that there was more matter here than met the eye. "Look in the shoes! Tear open the soles! And don't neglect to check every corner of this lute."

An officer went forward, reluctant to touch the dirty objects, but greed overcame his aversion. He checked the pockets, felt through carefully beneath the lining of the coat, ripped through the soles and the heels of the shoes. The only things he found were small pebbles in the shoes, and some bits of straw in the pockets of the jacket, and nothing but air inside the lute.

"These rags are decoys! He cannot cheat us like this! There is enough treasure here for all of us! Break through the walls, dig up the floor!" The emir's resolve to find something that would make Ayaz look bad in the king's eyes and at the same time fill his own coffers made him ignore the king's injunction not to make the search obvious to Ayaz.

With renewed zeal for their flagging hope, the officers went to it with picks, shovels, and hammers, ripping out the floor, ceiling, and walls. But all their efforts yielded nothing. Disappointed, tired, and covered with dust, they headed out to report to the king the next morning.

Meanwhile, the king had stayed awake all night considering his relationship with Ayaz. He couldn't find it in his heart to distrust Ayaz, and yet had a niggling doubt in his mind.

"O Ayaz," he spoke to him in his heart. "Even if you have done something, you are my beloved! Since you and I are one, it is I who has stolen treasure, and not you! I would bet my life that you are constant and loyal and the officers will find nothing! Forgive me for doubting you, my only friend."

Just as King Mahmoud finished his thought, Ayaz walked in simultaneously with the first light of dawn to serve and love his king. The king embraced him, and said, "Ayaz, my Ayaz, even if you should hear something today that sheds doubt on my love for you, know that I forgive you for anything you may have done or will ever do. And do you forgive me my doubt, and know that in my heart of hearts I know you are true!"

Before Ayaz could ask the king what he meant, the officers arrived, shamefaced and dejected. Not only were they proven wrong in their suspicions, but now they would fall out with the king and Ayaz as well. The king looked at the emir, who shook his head.

"Nothing, your majesty."

"Nothing?" the king asked.

"But this," said an officer, throwing down the rustic shoes and the patched up sheepskin jacket.

"They were hanging by an altar with a candle in it. There was also this lute hanging against a wall."

"Oh!" cried Ayaz, falling on his knees and cradling the objects in his arms. He held them near his heart and wept.

"Forgive me," said the king to Ayaz. And when Ayaz looked up at him, Mahmoud related to him what had transpired. "But tell me, my own soul, what is the significance of this jacket and these shoes, and why did you go to such pains to conceal these rags from everyone else? And why do you visit them every night, like a lover his mistress? And light a candle to them and sing ecstatic orisons to them?"

"It is my secret." Ayaz replied.

"What?" asked the king.

Ayaz was silent.

"When seeds are hidden in the earth, my lord," he said after a long pause, "they become the green of the earth. One needs to hide one's innermost treasure from the others," Ayaz said, kissing his jacket and shoes.

Everyone's ears perked up at the word "treasure."

"And why are these your treasure?"

Ayaz was silent a long time. His rivals hoped that there would still be a happy ending to their quest for riches, and Ayaz might finally reveal a secret hideaway in the objects that housed an invaluable ruby or pearl. "There is immense danger in all these riches and all this power you have given me, Sire," Ayaz said softly.

Was he finally going to confess he had been embezzling?

"What kind of danger? Tell these greedy officers once and for all if you have taken anything from my treasury."

"What need have I to take anything when you give me all I could ever want of material goods, and far more?"

The king's love for Ayaz, and his intense trust of him, gave way to a fierce rage towards his officers who had tried to besmear his beloved.

"Out of my sight—and out of my kingdom!" he yelled at them. "You have seen my beloved Ayaz in the mirror of your own greed. To fools such as you, gold and gems—which are to be scattered as an offering to the soul—appear more valuable than the soul. Go ahead and punish them, Ayaz! Kill them, or banish them. It is all one to me. I never want to see their faces again!"

"Forgive us!" said the emir, falling at Ayaz's feet.

"The fault, my king, is entirely mine," Ayaz replied. "I should not have given them occasion to doubt me. Forgive them, O ocean of pardon! And do not consign them to the hell of not being able to behold your face ever again!"

The officials and soldiers kissed Ayaz's feet, and left, like dogs with their tails between their legs. They would wonder forever about the reasons for Ayaz's secret worship of rags.

The king, burning with curiosity, turned to Ayaz and said, "Tell me, my Ayaz, tell me my beloved, why do you worship this worn out jacket and shoes?"

"They are the light of my life, my king," Ayaz replied. "I wear them every night as I sing in gratitude to Allah for the many, many gifts He has bestowed upon me. By reminding me of my poor beginnings, they keep me humble." ❧

# The Root of Treasure

MATHNAWI, VI, 1834-1989; 2256-2375

 AKIR SUFFERED GREATLY from poverty and hunger. Though he prayed and pleaded with God for help, none was forthcoming for many years. Being a reflective, contemplative, and thoughtful man, Fakir taught himself to be vigilant against his despair, to question and vanquish it the moment it arose. But it was not an easy battle.

In moments of hope he would pray passionately to God to fulfill his needs without his having to labor for them. "Oh you, who created me without any labor on my part, gave me my five senses to fend my way through and enjoy life, and so many innumerable gifts I cannot even count, please provide also for this stomach and body you have made. Nothing is beyond your power, Allah, so please also send me my daily bread."

But though he constantly struggled against despondency, Fakir often fell into it. In these dark times he would hear a voice saying to him, "Come!"

Then Fakir would understand the purpose of desperation and that all the changing and whirling conditions of the world and of his own mind, like peace and turmoil, faith and doubt, and all the other contraries, were part of God's plan for him and the world. But despite Fakir's philosophical attitude, his daily requirement for the necessities of life always brought him to his knees in prayer and supplication.

In a hungry, somnambulant state between waking and sleeping one morning, he heard the same voice say to him, "Go to the stationery store near the entrance to the mosque. In the pile of loose pages sold as models of good handwriting, you will find a scroll of pale yellow parchment frayed at the edges. Take it."

"Steal it?" Fakir asked with trepidation.

"Don't worry, it's yours," the voice replied. "Take it home and read it in the privacy of your home. Your dream is going to take a long time to fulfill, but do not be hasty, and do not despair. Endure the labor. All shall be well."

Fakir's joy knew no bounds, not only because his prayers were about to be fulfilled, but also because the voice was confirmation of an intelligent and intelligible power that answered prayers. God cared for and loved him! Fakir didn't need anything else!

But as the sun grew higher up in the sky, Fakir's stomach growled its hunger, and he found himself at the stationer's shop. Fakir found the stack of loose sheets, and before long his finger and eye happened upon the sheet described by the voice. His heart beat wildly, and when the stationer turned his back to him for a moment, Fakir slipped the paper into his pocket, and bidding goodbye to the shopkeeper, hurried to his house in a state of excitement.

"A treasure is buried outside town," Fakir read. "Go to the Martyr's domed shrine. Turn your back to the shrine, face the desert in the direction of Mecca, and release an arrow from your bow. Dig up the place where the arrow falls."

Fakir was at once happy and anxious. He wasn't a good archer! He had only played with a bow and arrow when he was a child, and had no skill in the weapon! Nevertheless, Fakir borrowed a strong bow and arrows, a pickaxe and a shovel, and headed out to the spot at early dawn so as to escape detection. It would not do to have the king find out about the scroll and claim the treasure for himself. Under the starlight and the waning moon,

Fakir stood with his back to the shrine, facing Mecca, mustered all his strength, and shot an arrow into the dark blue spaces beyond. He hurried with his implements to where the arrow had fallen, and quickly dug a hole before the early morning Muezzin's call, waking the town to prayer.

But Fakir found nothing. He did not despair, however, but determined to become better with the bow and the arrow. He hadn't found the treasure because of his poor skill in archery. He sold off his last belongings, and bought himself a stronger bow, better arrows, and practiced long and hard to improve his archery. Day by day he learned more, shot further and further with great strength, and increased in power and skill. But no matter how far he shot his arrows, when he dug up the place where they fell, he found nothing.

Fakir endured the toil, as he was told to do, practiced his skill, and persisted in building up his strength and his hope. But when some informers told the king that Fakir had found a scroll and was searching for treasure each morning outside town behind the Martyr's dome, the king summoned him. Fakir found himself once more in the grip of despair.

Fakir thought about running away and taking the scroll with him. He threw himself on the ground and was about to fall into the deepest despair at the failure of all his efforts when once again he heard the voice say to him, "Come!"

The sound was enough to rejuvenate Fakir. He rallied his flagging spirits, summoned his long-practiced wisdom, and knew what he must do: accept Allah's will, willingly. Before he could be arrested and imprisoned for not informing the king, Fakir knew he had to surrender the scroll to the king.

"I have found no treasure, sire," Fakir said, handing the scroll to the king, "but only a lot of labor and distress. But perhaps the treasure belongs to you, and you will be more successful in finding it."

The king summoned the most energetic and skilled archers from around the world, and dug up the desert yard-by-yard, inch-by-inch, wherever the arrows fell. But all his efforts were just as futile as Fakir's.

Weary of the search, and angry as well, the king returned the scroll to Fakir, and said, "It's all yours. You have nothing else to do, so seek it till the day you die. If you do not find it, you will have lost nothing, and if you do, it's all yours."

Relieved that he had been given the right of possession to the treasure, but not very hopeful of finding it—how could he be, when the best archers of the world had failed?—Fakir went into the desert in a melancholy, mad search for that power whose voice he had heard so often in his dreams and waking visions. A love was awakened in him that had nothing to do with any rewards. There was no need to go any further than his own heart to seek this treasure. Love was all the effort and the labor required of him. Love made him so intoxicated that his soul began to dance to the rhythm of: "Come! Come! Come!"

He fell to the ground in a swoon, and when he came to consciousness, a thought swam into his soul.

"Oh my beloved, you who are closer to me than my jugular vein, forgive me! I have labored hard and built up my strength, but never once did I ask your help in finding the treasure. I have been conceited and relied on my own strength. Today I go out with my bow and arrow in utter humility. Lead me to the root of this treasure."

Fakir walked slowly to the domed shrine, and once more stood in the appointed place. He shut his eyes and surrendered himself to the voice inside him that had pointed the way to the treasure. Once again he heard the voice: "You have shot the arrow of your thought too far, my friend. You were told to release the arrow from the bow, not pull the bowstring hard. Strip yourself of useless learning, vanity, cleverness so that the rain of divine mercy can fall on you. Go, do not shoot with all your strength, but be humble, soft, and trust in the might of Allah."

Fakir opened his eyes, put his arrow to the bow, and in a stance of meditative prayer released the arrow, which fell right by his feet, where he stood. He opened his eyes, kneeled to the ground and quietly dug up the soil and sand where he had been standing. And there, right there under his very feet, he found an ancient wooden chest full of gleaming gold. ✿

# VIII

# Befriend Death

The body is as a
garment to the spirit;
this arm is the sleeve
of the spirit's arm,
this foot the shoe
of the spirit's foot.

*MATHNAWI, III, 1609*

◇╫─◇─╫◇

The body is the
shadow
of the shadow
of the shadow of the
Heart.

*MATHNAWI, VI, 3307*

# Wings of the Wind

*MATHNAWI, I, 956-970*

NE MORNING AS the great ruler, Solomon, was sitting in his Hall of Justice, Shahed, one of the most eloquent poets of his court, ran into the hall and fell at Solomon's feet, muttering and blabbering incoherently. Everyone present was amazed and awestruck, for this man was the center of the intellectual circle of the court. People would travel long distances to hear his moving and impassioned recitations and philosophic discourses.

"Speak," said King Solomon. "What is the matter?"

Through chattering teeth and lips blue with terror, the poet said, "Save me! O save me!"

"From what shall I save you?" Solomon asked.

"The wind . . . in the street . . . outside, the wind," Shahed muttered and babbled, "cold, cold and horrible . . . wind, swords in my eyes, heart, belly . . . blades . . . death."

"It's all right, my man, it's all right, my beloved poet," King Solomon said, putting his hand on the Shahed's head, and calming him down. "Tell me."

"I . . . saw just now . . . as I was coming here . . . oh horrible . . . Azra'el in his black cloak, covering his face, only his eyes visible, piercing into my eyes like . . . daggers . . . so full of hatred and rage in the eyes of the Lord of Death. O my lord," Shahed said, falling to his knees and speaking with a fervor that loosened his tongue. "My lord, miracle-maker, supporter of the weak, O wise and wonderful king, save me, save me from the breath of Azra'el, the Angel of Death! I have so much more work to do . . . I am in the middle of my opus demonstrating how submission to God's will is superior to intellectual exertion and reliance upon our own efforts. You know, the one from which I recited quatrains only yesterday, the one everyone applauded, including you, my king. Buy me some time, and help me to finish it, I beg of you!"

"What shall I do?" Solomon asked.

"The wind is your slave. Command it to carry me across to India right away. Put an entire ocean between me and Azra'el, O lord!"

Solomon summoned the wind and commanded it to bear his favorite poet speedily across the seas and mountains to a remote and hidden place in the Himalayan jungles of India.

Later that day as Solomon held court, he saw Azra'el standing in the crowd before him. Solomon called him to his side, and asked, "Did you look with hatred at my poet this morning? He was very frightened."

"With hatred?" replied Azra'el. "Not in the least, my lord. I was merely astonished to see him here, for God had commanded me to take his life later today in India. And I thought to myself, even if he had the wind for wings, it will be impossible for him to reach India today." ✿

# The Prison and the Rose Garden

*MATHNAWI, I, 1547-1846*

HERE WAS ONCE a beautiful parrot, Misha, with a bright red beak, green, turquoise, and yellow feathers and lapis wings, who loved to sing and talk. She would fly about, free and joyous, in the mango groves of India, and in the rose gardens of kings. Once an old king heard Misha, and he and all his courtiers feasting in the garden, clapped in delight. Misha knew instinctively that the loud slapping together of hands was a compliment to her marvelous talent and the exquisiteness of her song. She fell in love with the sound of applause and would come daily to hear it after her singing, and to feed on the wonderful, exotic fruits the king left for her. But soon the old king died, and Misha flew west in search of more gardens and more kings to impress with her song and speech. All the kings who heard her, coveted her, but none was able to catch and cage her, except Nasser, a rich merchant from Baghdad.

Nasser was kind and generous, and treated the parrot very well. Misha was given a lovely mirror studded with diamonds, two gem-studded gold rings for her pretty feet, and all she could eat of the world's best fruits and nuts.

Before embarking on a business trip to India, Nasser asked his slaves and handmaidens what gifts they wanted from that country of exquisite objects.

"Ask for whatever you want," he said, magnanimously. "I expect to make a fortune there. Hopefully, I will also pick up some wisdom that will make my life more peaceful and joyous. Though I am rich and have everything anyone could ever desire, in my heart I feel a sickness with the ways of the world and with myself. I would like to find a way to be freer and happier."

His handmaidens and his slaves asked for pearls, emeralds, rubies, rings, and necklaces of lapis lazuli and turquoise, brocade, silk scarves, and shawls of expensive, rare wools, embroidered with threads of silver and gold. Nasser promised to bring them the objects of their desire.

"And you, my beautiful parrot, my sweet bird, my Misha, image of my soul, what would you like from India?" he asked. "Whatever you want, I shall bring for you. You have but to name it, and it shall be yours."

"I desire no thing," Misha replied. "But please, carry a message from me to the parrots of India. When you meet them, tell them: 'Misha, who I love and own, and who lives in a lovely cage made of tortoise shell, ivory, and gold, is sick with longing for you. She is weary of everything that has given her satisfaction and pleasure. Her soft, silken perch, exotic fruits, her lovely feathers, her vermilion beak, the words and songs she is so proud to speak and sing are empty and meaningless. Oh wise and free ones, who fly in the forests, orchards, and in rose gardens, think of her and drink a morning draft of tears amongst the meadows. Do not forget her, but hear the cry of her heart and send her a message that will give wings to her soul and make her soar once more in the blue skies of joy!'"

Misha said these words with so much anguish and passion that Nasser and the slaves felt tears welling up inside them. After wiping his tears, Nasser promised to deliver Misha's message to her sisters and brothers in India.

When Nasser reached India, he first went to the city to do business. He was very successful and acquired much wealth. He bought many expensive gifts for his slaves and handmaidens from the teeming, colorful bazaars of India. Then he went to the Indian countryside to relax at a fine resort before returning to his stressful businesses in Baghdad. One morning, as he sat in the orchard that was part of an expansive, rambling garden, he heard parrots chattering joyously as they ate the sweet fruits of the mango and guava trees. Nasser called out to the parrots, which fell silent and listened as he related Misha's message, word for word.

On hearing Nasser's message, one of the parrots sitting on a branch beat her wings wildly, turned still and rigid, and fell to the ground, dead. The kind merchant felt remorse that he had inadvertently caused the death of this beautiful bird. With sadness in his heart, he wondered what he was going to tell Misha.

On his return home Nasser distributed all the rich and wonderful gifts he had brought for his handmaidens and his slaves, but said nothing to Misha. But his parrot, who had been waiting anxiously for some word from the parrots of India, said: "Where is my gift? What message did you bring for me from my sisters in India?"

"None," replied Nasser. "I delivered your message but they said nothing."

"Tell me what you saw and heard," she said.

"I don't know why you gave me such a disturbing message. I'm sorry that I delivered it to them."

"O master, tell me what causes you so much repentance and grief? I long to hear," Misha said passionately.

"I repeated your words to a flock of parrots that resembled you. One of them was so anguished that she fluttered her wings in agitation, trembled, fell, and died."

When Misha heard what her sister had done, she too, shuddered, collapsed, and died.

The distraught merchant dashed his cap to the ground and tore his clothes in grief. "My beautiful Misha, with your sweet voice and song, my confidante, I have killed you. Why did I so thoughtlessly tell you what I saw in India? My business, work, money is useless to me without you. Oh, what an unhappy man I am! This world is a prison to me without you, my winged friend, my soul."

Then gently, he opened the cage, took out his bird, already still and rigid in death, and put her on the sill of an open window, sobbing and keening in sorrow. As he wiped his tears and blew his nose, with a sudden and quick fluttering of her wings, Misha flew away to a high branch of a palm tree in the garden.

Nasser was awestruck as he saw the colors and beauty of her wings, which he had never seen in flight before. He lifted up his face and said, "Misha, my beautiful parrot, explain this mystery to me before you go! What did you learn from the parrot in India that made you do this dreadful thing to me?"

"My sister from India showed me how to be free: Give up being proud of your song and voice; abandon your clever words and your lust for applause that has imprisoned you in your cage of gold. Live as one dead, to gain release."

Having said this, Misha flew up into the blue sky, her lapis wings fluttering and shining with light.

"Ah," said Nasser. "My wise friend, farewell. May God protect you in your freedom. And may I, too, learn from you how to live this life with more joy and freedom." ♆

# The Eye of the Heart

MATHNAWI, III, 1772-1835; 1924-2305; 3399-3418

 certain, wise Sheikh lost both his sons to the ravages of disease, but no one ever saw him lamenting and complaining. He went about his business cheerfully from day to day, singing at his tasks as before.

The Sheikh's family observed him, and one morning at breakfast, while the Sheikh was eating his bread and drinking his salted tea, they couldn't control themselves any longer.

The Sheikh's mother said to him: "Son, we are broken by our loss. Our hearts and minds are torn and bleeding. We cannot eat, drink, or sleep. Your wife is becoming thin as a hair. Look at her! But you . . . do you even realize what has happened? You go about your business as if, as if . . ." She could go no further. She broke down and sobbed quietly.

"You are a heartless, pitiless man!" burst his wife, venting in rage all her grief upon her husband. "Not a sob, not a tear did you shed, you unfeeling man! You did not love our little ones, otherwise wouldn't you mourn and lament? And you go about life as if, as if they are still alive and nothing has changed!"

"Nothing has changed my dear wife. Dead or alive, our sons are never absent or invisible from the eye of my heart."

"I look around every nook and cranny, I lie awake at night because I imagine them crying for me outside. 'Amma,' they cry,

'Amma, take us inside, we are cold and hungry.' I strain my eyes in the dark to find them, but they are gone! Nowhere! Nowhere! Where is this eye of the heart that can show them to me once more, so I can hold them to my breast and feel their hearts beating next to mine! The eye of your heart! It is a single, blind eye!"

"It is single, beloved, and not blind. Our two eyes mislead us into thinking in a double way. Here, there, now, then, present, absent—there is no separation for me. I see our beloved sons all the time. They are playing all around me."

"Where? Show me! My eyes don't see them anywhere."

"That's because these physical eyes veil reality, beloved. Our senses are like weeds on clear water. Your spirit, if you trust it, can sweep those weeds away and help you see further than your eyes can see. Shut your eyes, put your senses to sleep so you may awaken to the Unseen and embrace our sons again."

"But my arms are empty! Empty!" She cried, hugging her own breast and then beating her belly with her fists.

"We don't understand all this business about some other eye that sees some things other than the things that are," his mother replied. "We are simple people, not learned like you. Do not confuse us with your philosophy."

The Sheikh felt impatient with his mother and wife, and wanted to return to his tasks and leave them to their misery.

"We have always looked up to you," his mother continued. "People say you are like a shepherd, guiding them, but you have no pity in your heart for your own family. Mourn with us, son, so your heart may share and lighten some of our grief, for we are suffering beyond endurance."

The Sheikh was silent a long time. His impatience turned to sadness when he realized that his mother and wife could not partake of his reality, that he could do nothing to help them in their sorrow. They couldn't see what he saw because their minds, fed by their eyes, created and perpetuated separation. He knew that this, and not death, was the real tragedy that caused their suffering.

"There was a woman who lost every child she bore in the first few months after birth," the Sheikh began, hoping to divert them by a story.

"Yes, at least we had our little ones for some years," his mother said, wiping her tears with the end of her veil.

"What happened to the woman?" the wife asked. "Did she die of her grief? I have heard people can die of sorrow. Oh, how I want to die, too!"

"In the beginning, she wanted to die as well. 'For nine months I bear the burden of pregnancy, and for a few months I have joy, and then I am plunged into despair again. My joy is more fleeting than a rainbow!' she cried."

The women sobbed at the analogy.

"Twenty children she lost this way," the Sheikh continued. "Not two, but twenty!"

"How . . . how could she bear it?" they cried.

"She cried and cursed Allah loudly in the streets. The mullah and the people said to her, 'Perhaps these afflictions are sent to you so you may take refuge with Allah in your hour of need.' But she was too full of grief to do anything for herself.

"One night she had a vision. As she slithered through a desert, her open, wounded belly bleeding upon the sands, her throat parched with a fierce thirst, the full moon rained its light upon her like grace. A narrow gate appeared before her. She lifted herself up with much effort and slid through it like a child through a tight birth canal. With new eyes, she saw what even our best poets are unable to describe. The only words and images that reach us from that other side are 'Salsabil, the fountain of eternal life, and Kawthar, the river of Paradise flowing through a Garden with undying flowers and trees.'"

"Not like our gardens, in which plants die and never return," the Sheikh's mother mourned.

"It is the Garden no eye has ever seen. It is visible to those who believe and trust. It is the source, my dear ones, of all the gardens that give us such joy."

"It doesn't exist!" cried his wife. "Except in your fantasies!"

"This garden, beloved, is the metaphor for that which has no name and cannot be described. Believe me, it exists."

"But what happened to the woman who lost all her children? What good is a garden without children?"

"She stepped into the gentle, healing waters of Kawthar, and all her grief and doubt washed away like dirt and grime. As she splashed the water into her eyes and ears she heard the delightful laughter of children close by. And there they were, all her children, all around her, swimming, laughing, and splashing about in the fountain of God's heart."

The women wept at this picture.

"God took her grieving heart and replaced it with a joyous one. In the midst of mourning, she was given festivity."

"But how do I get there? How do I do it?" his wife cried.

"The saints, my dear ones, never object to anything that happens to them or the people around them. They know that far greater things are given than those taken away. Some saints do not even open their mouths to ask Allah for anything. They consider it infidelity to Allah to seek to avert destiny. Their delight lies in submission to destiny. They never put on the blue garb of mourning."

"How can we submit to a will that is so harsh?" his wife cried. "Not just one, but both of them, within a few days of each other!"

"It is not easy. Even Daquqi doubted."

"We do not know who this Daquqi fellow is, and we don't care," his wife said sullenly.

"Now listen to a story of those travelers on the Path who do not object to any event or circumstance. They just watch it all."

"Tell us, son, for your stories bring comfort to our hearts," his mother said, picking up a piece of bread, chewing it, and washing it down with a gulp of tea.

"Daquqi was a pilgrim on the Earth, always moving from place to place so as not to get attached to people or places."

"Not attached? How unnatural."

"He did have an attachment."

"To his children?" his wife asked, eagerly.

"No, to saints. He was bound to them with an irrepressible hunger and desire. He learned from them, and they took his hand and led him to the garden of Paradise where his heart was opened to the wonder of this world and the next. In the prophets and saints he could see the ocean in a drop of water, and the sun in a mote. Through them he could behold divinity in all humans.

"He roamed, barefoot over stones and thorns, searching for saints. If anyone said to him, 'Daquqi, your feet are bleeding!' he would say to them, 'Do not regard these feet that walk on the earth, for the lover of God walks on his heart.'

"One day as he was journeying, he arrived at a shore. The sea stretched in one direction, and sand and dunes in the other. The sun had set, and the blue sky had turned to a dark indigo, which made a few stars visible. Like dawn, it was the magical time of day, a threshold and a doorway to the other, invisible world. In the distance Daquqi saw seven tall candles, taller than the tallest palm trees, casting a bright light all around them. He hastened toward the light, walked for many hours, and found himself in a village. Hundreds of people walked the street with unlit lamps, moaning and groaning, grumbling and weeping.

'Why are you so sullen and sad?' Daquqi asked a young man.

'Can't you see?' the man snapped. 'We have no oil or wicks for our lamps, and no food or drink for our bellies.'

'But look! The sky is so bright! The light of these candles is falling all around us like rain! Just look! God gives light without any lamp!' Daquqi cried in amazement.

'What light? It is a pitch-black night,' the man replied, looking at Daquqi as if he were mad. Daquqi looked at the man and saw that his eyes, like the eyes of all the others who were stumbling about in the dark, were sewn shut, even though they appeared to be wide open.

"Daquqi looked at the candles and before his eyes the seven candles merged to become one candle, and then again, divided into seven candles.

"Daquqi sat and watched for a long time, wondering at the spectacle that only he seemed to be seeing. He sat till it was day again, and still the seven candles glowed so brightly that even daylight seemed pale and murky before it. The sun climbed higher in the sky; the desert became blindingly bright and burning hot.

"Before Daquqi's amazed eyes, the seven candles became seven trees so lush that Daquqi's eyes feasted on their greenery. They were laden with a strange, yellow fruit, all within easy reach. Daquqi moved from the hot desert into their cool, breezy shade. He plucked and ate a fruit. It burst its sweet juice in his mouth.

"But what truly amazed Daquqi was that the hundreds of people in the village made parasols out of torn garments to protect themselves from the blazing sun, and they couldn't see or feel the shade of the trees. And they were groaning with hunger and thirst in the midst of a feast!

"Without tongues the trees were saying to the people, 'O come to us, you unfortunate ones!'

"Daquqi shouted to them angrily, 'Look, the trees in the garden are calling to you! Eat and drink in their cool shade!'

'We don't see anything,' they muttered, rubbing their eyes. 'There is no garden here, but an unending desert. Go away, you fool. We are leaving this barren village by that ship on the sea to find a better place to live. Even if we drown in the ocean, we will be better off than here.'

'You are so blind! You keep feeding each other and yourselves the same, bitter lies!' Daquqi exclaimed.

'Be quiet,' even the intelligent amongst them said. 'You are infecting and deluding us with your folly, for we have glimpses of a garden orchard, but it is only a vain dream, and we must return to what is rational and real.'

'What is real?' Daquqi asked. 'Hunger and thirst and scorching sunshine? You hunger and thirst for half a rotten grape, when you can have wholesome fruit bursting with nourishing juice?'

'We will find a better place across the seas,' they said.

"But when even the acute amongst the hundreds of people doubted, Daquqi, too, began to doubt. 'Am I mad?' He wondered. 'Are they right and am I wrong?' For a long time Daquqi doubted till he began to feel deranged. Then he went up to a tree, touched it, and ate the fruit. 'But I can touch these trees, feel their cool shade, eat their fruit. Yes, perhaps I am a fool, but I prefer my fruitful madness to their barren intelligence,' he said to himself.

"But Daquqi felt sad, very sad that he couldn't help all these people in their misery, for he was a compassionate man who prayed to alleviate the suffering of mankind, and was kind to the good and bad alike.

"Before Daquqi's eyes the trees moved and arranged themselves in a single line, with one tree before them, like an Imam before his congregation of men about to begin their prayers. The trees bowed down without knees or waists and began to pray. Just then the seven trees turned to seven men, all seated in contemplation.

"Daquqi approached them and they said, 'O Daquqi, glory and crown of the Noble!'

'But . . . how did you know my name?' Daquqi asked in wonderment.

'Nothing is hidden from the heart that longs for God. We share one heart, Daquqi,' one of the men replied. 'You think in terms of individual hearts, but there is only one heart, a single heart, God's. Leave the fragment and come to the whole!'

"Daquqi broke down and wept tears of joy for he had found what we had been seeking for so long! A community of saints, of like-hearted people. He had come home! He was happy, happy, happy! He wanted to stay with them forever!

'Come, lead us in prayer, Daquqi,' they said.

'But I am . . . a crazy fool,' Daquqi replied.

'Your eyes and heart are clear. The clear sighted, clear hearted fool is superior to all the others.'

"In all humility, Daquqi led the prayer. They all fell into a deep state of communion where their souls merged with each other's and with God's. No identity or personality remained. The many became one and duality was obliterated. No search or seeker remained. Time itself, which creates duality and which births, ages, and kills us with it revolutions, came to a halt. They sat thus all day long and late into the night."

The Sheikh, who had been narrating Daquqi's story, fell into a deep trance, and was silent for a long time. He was brought back to the present by the cry of his wife.

"Where, oh where is such a place where I, too, can merge with my children! Tell me! Teach me! O Allah, I who have not thought about you at all, help me now, for I am sinking!"

The Sheikh opened his eyes and saw his wife rocking back and forth, her face contorted in grief so inconsolable, so impermeable to remedy, that the Sheikh, who had been disturbed at being transported back so suddenly to such a sight of sorrow, was filled to the brim with compassion.

"And then what happened, son?" the Sheikh's mother asked, gently.

"While Daquqi was in the very thick of meditation, he heard screams and shouts and cries of distress and fear. While the seven men continued to pray, ignoring the cries and letting Allah take care, or not, of whoever needed help, Daquqi opened his eyes and looked. In a little light from the moon almost obscured by dark clouds, he saw a sea in agitated turmoil. Huge waves rose and fell, and upon it tossed and twirled a ship with hundreds on board. Its mast was broken, its sail in tatters, its bow already half sunken into the raging sea. The people were desperately clinging to the railing to keep themselves from sliding down into the waters. They clung to each other out of fear. Neither their intelligence nor their grasp of 'reality' helped them. Faced with their own death, they realized the value of life and their need for Allah's invaluable aid. All of them, who had never before even thought about or believed in Allah, prayed to Him in their hour of need: 'Help us! Save us!'

"Suddenly Daquqi heard a loud crack. The ship had broken into two, and the people were plunged up to their throats in briny water.

"Daquqi's heart was swept up in a storm of compassion and pity, and tears flowed from his eyes. He felt for the people as a mother would for her children. His heart burst out into a silent, impassioned prayer: 'O Lord, give them your hand and save them. O merciful one, forgive them their ignorance. Oh free those who live in the prison of the senses, of direction, and time and space! Save them, draw them out of the clay and teach them to devote themselves to the saints, who are the lords of the heart. Open their eyes and lead them to the garden of your paradise, Allah!'"

At this point in the story the Sheikh broke down and wept copiously, the briny tears flowing out of him in a torrent. He did not know whom he was weeping for—his mother, his wife, his lost children, himself, the people in the ship, or for all the broken hearts of this world. He only knew that the weeping was a release and a gift.

A long silence followed the Sheikh's prayer in Daquqi's words, and his sobbing. His wife felt a flood of relief, as if the burden of her sorrow was lightened somehow.

"Were they saved, son?" His mother asked.

"Yes. The chosen servants of God, the saints, possess the powers of Allah to put things right and to help in the heavy, grievous day. The breath of the saint's prayer is enough. The sea became calm at once, and each one of them survived. They swam ashore on fragments of the ship just as daylight broke upon the shore, flooding everything with light. Calamity had opened their eyes and washed their hearts clean of disbelief and despair."

Another long silence followed.

"That is the function and reason of tragedy, my dear ones," the Sheikh said, quietly.

The Sheikh's wife reached for a piece of bread, put it in her mouth, and drank some water. She ate and drank in silence, then took the utensils and began to wash them.

"Was that the end of the story?" the Sheikh's mother asked.

"No. The spiritual journey is not easy, Mother. Like fools we keep forgetting, keep stumbling on the same bump on the Way.

We have to continue to learn, and relearn again and again and again."

"Tell me the rest of the story, Son."

"The prayer was over simultaneously as the people were rescued. The seven men opened their eyes and looked towards the sea." As the Sheikh continued the story, his wife, too, left the dishes and sat by him to listen.

"All at once the seven men looked at each other and wondered: 'Who is the busy body who meddled with destiny?' They could tell by looking at Daquqi that he was the one. Suddenly, all seven of them disappeared into thin air, their light merging with the light all around. Daquqi found himself all alone on the shore once more.

"Daquqi fell into deep despair over his separation from the men whose company he had traveled far and wide for a long, long time to find. For many years he roamed, shedding tears of longing for them, and blaming himself.

"Then one night he looked into a well, and saw the reflection of the full moon in it. It was so beautiful that Daquqi broke into a song and dance in its praise. But a cloud obscured the moon and its reflection vanished from the water. Exhausted and despairing, Daquqi lay down on the sand by the well, and looked up at the sky. Suddenly he sat up and hit himself over his head with his hands.

'Stupid, stupid, stupid Daquqi! Infidel, Daquqi! Ignorant Daquqi! You have been worshiping an idol, a mere reflection! Wear the saints' words as a garment, you fool; stitch their words to your heart! Leave the fragment, and come to the whole. God gives light without any lamp—if your lamp is gone, why are you lamenting? You thought the seven men were human beings. How long will you regard this external form? How long? How long? How long will you be bound to your senses and your eyes? How long will you worship phantoms? Daquqi, oh fool, Daquqi! Remember to remember!'"

The Sheikh's words lingered in the humble cottage for a long time. Then all three of them got up and quietly returned to the tasks of the day. ❧

# Sources

ll thirty stories in *Rumi's Tales from the Silk Road* have their source in the six books that comprise *The Mathnawi of Jalalu'din Rumi*, edited and translated by Reynold A. Nicholson (Cambridge, England: The Trustees of the E.J.W. Gibb Memorial in association with Book Production Consultants, 1982 edition).

The volume and verse numbers of the original story as it appears in the *Mathnawi* are listed under the name of each story's respective title in this work.

In addition, I have consulted various reference guides for Muslim saints ("Bayazid's Holy Body") and the Bible for the stories on Jesus and Joseph ("Bones" and "The Gift"). While writing the preface, I consulted Camille and Kabir Helmminski's introduction in *Rumi: Daylight* (Boston: Shambala, 2000), *Teachings of Rumi* by Andrew Harvey (Boston: Shambala, 1999), *The Way of the Sufi* by Indries Shah (New York: E.P. Dutton, 1970), and *Tales from the Land of Sufis* by Mojdeh Dayat and Mohammad Ali Jamnia (Boston: Shambala, 1994).

# Acknowledgements

hanks are due first of all to my husband, Payson R. Stevens, for his almost tireless reading and rereading of these stories; to the late Jon Phetteplace for bequeathing the *Mathnawi* through Payson to me; to my late father, Brig. Hardit Singh Kapur, for encouraging and inspiring me to explore all religions; and last but not least, to Raoul Goff and the wonderful crew at Mandala for their continuing support.